Charles Voysey

The Testimony of the Four Gospels Concerning Jesus Christ

Charles Voysey

The Testimony of the Four Gospels Concerning Jesus Christ

ISBN/EAN: 9783743395060

Manufactured in Europe, USA, Canada, Australia, Japa

Cover: Foto ©Lupo / pixelio.de

Manufactured and distributed by brebook publishing software (www.brebook.com)

Charles Voysey

The Testimony of the Four Gospels Concerning Jesus Christ

THE TESTIMONY OF THE FOUR GOSPELS CONCERNING JESUS CHRIST.

BY THE

REV. CHARLES VOYSEY, B.A.,

ST. EDMUND HALL, OXFORD; FORMERLY VICAR OF HEALAUGH, YORKSHIRE; MINISTER OF THE THEISTIC CHURCH.

WILLIAMS AND NORGATE,
14, HENRIETTA STREET, COVENT GARDEN, LONDON;
20, SOUTH FREDERICK STREET, EDINBURGH;
AND 7, BROAD STREET, OXFORD.
1896.

Price Three Shillings and Sixpence.

TABLE OF CONTENTS.

	PAGE
PREFACE	v.

LECTURE I.
INTRODUCTORY 1

LECTURE II.
SOURCES OF OUR KNOWLEDGE 13

LECTURE III.
SERMON ON THE MOUNT 26

LECTURE IV.
CHRIST AS A MIRACULOUS HEALER . . 39

LECTURE V.
NOT PEACE, BUT A SWORD. 52

LECTURE VI.
DR. MARTINEAU'S EULOGY EXAMINED . 73

LECTURE VII.
SAME, CONTINUED. 84

LECTURE VIII.
GROUNDS OF HOSTILITY OF THE CONTEMPORARIES OF CHRIST 96

LECTURE IX.
THE GOOD TEACHINGS OF CHRIST . . 109

LECTURE X.
THE BAD TEACHINGS 122

LECTURE XI.
CHRIST AS A BARRIER BETWEEN GOD AND MEN . 136

LECTURE XII.
MY OWN EULOGY OF CHRIST 149

LECTURE XIII.
CORROBORATIVE TESTIMONY IN THE ACTS OF THE APOSTLES 160

LECTURE XIV.
DEFENCE OF THE CONTROVERSY . . . 172

PREFACE.

THIS book is sure to bring down fresh obloquy upon myself and upon the sacred cause which I aspire to serve. It is therefore necessary to guard against misunderstandings and misrepresentations at the outset. In as few words as possible, I wish to state what the object of this book is and what it is not.

To begin with the negative, my object here is not to attack, or to depreciate in the very smallest degree, that ideal of human goodness and even perfection which is so widely identified throughout Christendom with the name of Jesus Christ. We cannot have too lofty and pure an ideal of what man may and ought to reach, and in thousands of Christian hearts that ideal is associated with the name of Christ. To them the name of Jesus Christ stands for the most perfect man in all relations of life, the most perfect father, most perfect son, and most perfect brother; no less for the most perfect woman, mother, daughter and sister; all that is sweetest and best in human relations, in conduct and in character, is typified or symbolised to the mind under the term "Christ-like."

To be like Christ is understood as equivalent to reaching the highest ideal of goodness, and being worthily acceptable to God.

I need not dilate upon this. Every true-hearted Christian will know what I mean and cordially respond to it. Now, nothing can be farther from my wish or from the purpose of this book than to diminish by one tittle that reverence for a high and noble ideal of human conduct and character, or to revile or assail or even criticise *that* Christ which is so taken for a supreme model and which confers the name "Christian" upon the loveliest conception of human virtues.

Neither would I do or say anything to weaken the holy and benign influences of believing in the friendliness and love of the ideal Jesus Christ when regarded as an ever-present divine person standing, in fact, as God and in the place of God, a perfect substitute for God to the soul which knows no better, never had a chance to learn any better, about the One living and loving God who made and loves us all. The magnanimity of God grants a bounteous indulgence to all who earnestly cast themselves upon His love and mercy under any form and with any human name that may have become inevitable and indispensable to the life and health of the soul.

We Theists know full well that our use of the term "God" instead of "Christ" gives us no warrant for the monstrous assumption that we *know* God any better for calling Him God. It is not the name we give to our supreme and only object of worship and trust and love which divides us from Christians or gives us the slightest advantage over them in the sight of God. In whatsoever we have a real advantage it is due only to our having a truer and nobler conception of God's mind and dealings with our race. So here again it must be noted that this book is not issued against those who believe in a supreme God of love and justice and compassion, but who call that God by the name of Christ.

So much for the negative statement of the purposes of this book.

Its object is really this:

To prove, out of the Four Gospels themselves, that the beautiful ideal of a perfected humanity which devout Christians cherish is *not* identical with the Jesus Christ who is described in the Gospels, but is unspeakably higher and nobler than the Christ of the Gospels, and that it is naturally depraving to their own ideal of perfection, to go on infatuated with the notion that the portrait of Jesus Christ in the Gospels corresponds with it.

I wish to stop once and for all the inflated language about the unique perfection of Christ and his teachings, which is used not to denote an imaginary Christ of pious sentiment, but the historical Christ as depicted in the Gospels. This is the fatal error which must be uprooted if either religion or morality is to be saved and placed on solid foundations.

For this purpose, I herein simply draw attention to what the Gospels record as the words and deeds of Jesus Christ. Hitherto, familiarity with those records has totally obscured the devout reader to the errors in doctrine and to the moral blemishes which those Gospels ascribe to Jesus Christ. I have, it is true, interspersed my own comments among the quotations. But those comments could all be wiped out without in the least degree affecting the argument or the object of this book. Whatever truth and force it may contain is due only to the quotations from the Gospels. I assert that if religious people will give fair attention to those quotations, their moral sense will for the first time—possibly *not* for the first time—receive a shock, and they will be compelled to seek some relief from their perplexity. The ordinary plan is simply a dishonest, a dishonourable plan, viz.: to try to explain the words away or to substitute words which convey an exactly opposite meaning. This has become a characteristic vice among the defenders of the Gospels, who do not shrink from applying to those books a method of so-called interpretation which would be denounced even by themselves as grossly unfair and immoral in dealing with any other documents in the world.

For great plainness of speech, with one or two rare exceptions, the language of the Gospels is absolutely lucid, and needs no interpretation at all; and no one has ever been able to explain away the words in the Gospels ascribed to Jesus Christ in which he proclaimed his belief in Devils, the division of mankind into the saved and the lost, and the endlessness of future punishment.

It does not make it any more true because it is the fashion, to deny that Christ taught everlasting punishment. *Litera scripta manet*, and while the Gospels endure, the witness they bear to Christ's teaching on this point is unshakable.

In *The Christian Doctrine of Immortality*, by the Rev. Professor Salmond, he devotes chapter VI to the "Doctrine of Final Destinies," wherein he gives the most masterly and exhaustive examination to the teachings of Christ on endless punishment. The following words of the Professor are well worthy of attention :—

> Christ's own teaching, we must conclude, gives the significance of finality to the moral decisions of the present life. If there are possibilities of change, forgiveness, relaxation of penalty, or cessation of punishment in the future life, His words, at least, do not reveal the case. He never softens the awful responsibilities of this life, even by the dim adumbration of such possibilities. His recorded sayings nowhere suggest the provision of ministries of grace, whether now or continued in the after-existence. They nowhere speak of repentance unto life in

the other world. They nowhere open the prospect of remedial discipline in the disembodied state, or of terminable award in the conditions which follow the great day. They bring the two events, death and judgment, into relation, and give no disclosure of an intermediate state with untold potentialities of divine love and human surrender.

The truths of the resurrection, the judgment and the last awards, by which faith has held through all the Christian centuries, are all recognised in their broad features in Christ's own words . . . . the truths themselves are in Christ's teaching.

. . . . . .

The testimony of the Gospels, read with an open eye in the light of the history of Jewish thought, remains what we have found it to be; and there are but two ways of disposing of it, short of frank and reverent acceptance. One way is to take it as the record, reliable so far as it goes, of imperfect recollections of Christ's words—an honest but partial and mistaken apprehension of Christ's meaning, a record of the mind of the Evangelists as ascribed to Christ, rather than of Christ's mind as reported by the Evangelists. The other is to take it as a true account of Christ's words and a just representation of His meaning, and seek relief from it by assuming a philosophical superiority to it, and treating it as a provisional form of truth, or an accommodation to the limited ideas of the period and the country. Either way is a confession that Christ's teaching, as it comes to us in the evangelical narratives, contains those solemn truths of the Divine judgment of men and the eternal awards—(pages 389, 390, 391, 392.)

This book of mine makes it clear that as a teacher of theology the Jesus Christ of the Four Gospels was greatly mistaken, and, as an example for us to follow, by no means perfect, and that it would be an abuse of terms to call him Lord or Saviour or Master, being so much open to criticism and objection.

Moreover, it cannot be too often repeated that I am in no sense responsible for a single word, good or bad, true or false, found in the Gospels. And if not responsible, therefore I am not in the least deserving of blame for simply directing attention to what the Gospels contain.

This book is needed especially by those who have no access to the results of modern criticism, and neither learning nor leisure to study them. They are mainly the privilege of scholars, while the people at large are systematically taught in the schools and from the pulpits the same old beliefs and conceptions of the infallibility of the New Testament, without the faintest allusion to the results of modern criticism.

My present endeavour is to help the ordinary folk to see for themselves what is only too easy to see, without the cumbrous machinery of high scholarship.

I believe I have done my imperative duty. I know I have tried to do it, and I care neither for praise nor blame. "With me it is a very small thing that I should be judged of you or of man's judgment; yea, I judge not mine own self. But he that judgeth me is my God."

CHARLES VOYSEY.

St. Valery, Hampstead, N.W.
July, 1896.

P.S.—It is necessary to refer here to Rev. Dr. Martineau's essay, *Five Points of Christian Faith*, which I have criticised in Lectures VI—XII. That essay was advertised in *The Inquirer* without any date, as though it were a new publication, and I procured it accordingly for use in my controversy with the Unitarians. Some months later Dr. Martineau wrote to me saying that the essay was written fifty-four years ago, and was purposely omitted from the collection of *Essays, Reviews and Addresses* recently republished by him, because that essay was "out of date." He says to me "I am *morally* with you, and only *historically* against you," and he refers to his book on *The Seat of Authority in Religion*, as more accurately describing his present position.

Lecture I.

INTRODUCTION.

In the year 1871, shortly after the beginning of the work of The Theistic Church in London, I preached seven Sermons entitled: *What think ye of Christ?* These were republished in the fifth volume of *The Sling and the Stone*. Although there is much in those Sermons which I could repeat sincerely to-day, there is also much in them which I could not repeat, because I know more than I did then, because my mind has been growing in strength and clearness, and because the critical and sentimental literature on the subject of Jesus Christ demands a fresh examination of the claims made by him or on his behalf. I have therefore instructed my literary executor not to republish those Sermons of 1871 without the most careful excision of those passages which I could not now honestly repeat.

You do not need to be reminded how often the subject of Christ has been brought before you, and how intense have been the feelings of pain and repugnance which my words have aroused in some few of my hearers and readers. About twenty years ago I was entreated by a learned member of our Church to write a new history of Jesus Christ. But my reply to him, and to others who had asked for it likewise, amounted to this: "I have no sources whatever for a new history of Christ. The only sources which I believe to exist are the Four Gospels of the New Testament, and the first chapter of the Acts of the Apostles. I cannot go outside these documents which are quite as accessible to you and to everybody else as they are to me. Contemporary history is as absolutely silent about Jesus Christ as though he had never lived at all. All I can hope to do is to point out to you what these documents allege, and to fasten your attention upon passages which you have perhaps forgotten, or you have never clearly seen what they actually say." And to-day I cannot retract one word of that negative statement about the sources of our knowledge of Christ.

But the later criticisms of the Gospels, notably in the very learned work, recently published by Messrs. Williams & Norgate, entitled *The Four Gospels as Historical Records*, enable me to add something to that reply of mine, and to say now, that those sources of the only knowledge of Christ attainable at all are now discovered to be all but worthless as historical records; that we can hardly depend upon them with certainty for the accuracy of any narrative even of the most ordinary event, and cannot at all depend upon them for the accuracy of any words attributed to Christ in the Gospels. And surely these facts, if they be facts and not untruths, manifestly put the knowledge of the real Jesus Christ further off than ever. The more the Gospels are shown to be untrustworthy, the less able we are to discern or to determine the real truth about the real Jesus.

Now, if this uncertainty surrounded the life and sayings of anybody else, *e.g.*, Gautama Buddha, Moses or Mahommed, to the Christian world it would be a matter of no importance at all. And if it were of no importance to them, it would be of no importance to us Theists, it would give rise to no excitement of feeling on either side, therefore to no controversy or need for it. But Jesus Christ stands in Christendom in altogether a unique position. The three great Churches, the Greek, the Roman and the Anglican, all the Protestant Churches and Sects of Europe, America and the Colonies, the Lutherans, Presbyterians, Baptists, Wesleyans and Congregationalists and all the minor sections into which they have been subdivided—all agree in holding that Jesus Christ was verily a God on earth, that he is co-equal and co-eternal with Almighty God the Creator of the world and the Father of all souls. The majority of these Churches and Sects believe also that Jesus Christ is the only Saviour from everlasting Hell, the only Mediator between God and man, the only Intercessor who enables or persuades God to listen to our prayers. Moreover, all these Christian Churches and Sects believe that Jesus Christ lived and died on earth as a perfectly faultless human being, that every word he spake was true, and every precept and example of his were divine rules for our conduct and patterns for our imitation. Finally, they all profess to believe that Jesus Christ will some day return to this our planet, in the human body wherewith he ascended into heaven, to judge all mankind both quick and dead.

There is, however, a comparatively small though influential Sect who call themselves Christians, who do not believe in the Deity of Jesus Christ or in the orthodox sense of his being a Saviour from Hell, or in his final return to judgment. But this Sect (known as Unitarians), for reasons of their own into which we need not now enquire, persist in calling themselves Christians, and claim the right to be so regarded; many of them insisting that the life and words of Jesus were so exceptionally superior to those of all other men as to entitle him to the rank of Divinity—not quite so high as Deity, but so vastly higher than other men as to be practically superhuman or divine. This Jesus Christ is asserted by Unitarians to have brought into the world the best and most lofty conceptions of God which the world had ever heard, that his "revelation" of the mind and heart of God was so far above every other that Jesus Christ stands by himself on a pinnacle, not exactly to be worshipped as God, but to have his name alone coupled with God's Name in prayer, and to have Hymns written and sung in his praise—all this on the score of Christ's alleged superhuman and unique perfection and the super-excellence of his teaching. Of course to those who regard this as a pure invention of the human fancy, and who have no sources of any knowledge of Christ outside the New Testament, the Unitarian position naturally seems irrational; and they reply to the Unitarian on this wise, How can you call Jesus a perfect man or say that he is the highest religious teacher when such and such are recorded as his words in the Gospels? The Unitarian reply is to this effect: "We admit that these passages are moral and religious blemishes; but we do not believe that Jesus Christ ever spoke those objectionable words." In plain English, the Unitarians accept, as accurate historical reports, all the good and true sayings put into Christ's lips in the Gospels, and reject, as unhistorical and unveracious reports, all the sayings ascribed to him which are not morally and religiously blameless. I am convinced that this is utterly indefensible. Nevertheless, I myself have no hesitation in saying that I also disbelieve that Jesus Christ said certain words ascribed to him in the Gospels; yet not on the ground that they are merely bad, but on the ground that they are so bad that no ordinary human being, much less a professed teacher of religion, could possibly have uttered them. As examples of these outrageously impossible utterances are those wherein Jesus says that he speaks to the common people in parables in order to mislead them and prevent their repentance and conversion; and that other passage in which he affirms that the express purpose of his coming was not to bring peace but a sword, was to set fathers and mothers against their children, and children against their parents, and to sow strife in the home.* I only disbelieve that Jesus Christ said such things because they are too bad to impute to any human being at all. Of such passages there are happily only a few. My rejection of them is therefore not parallel to the Unitarian method of rejecting *all* the passages to which any moral objection may be taken. If the Unitarians had other sources of correct information wherewith to test the accuracy of the Gospels, that would alter the whole case; but, after accepting the Gospels as their only source of all knowledge of Christ whatever, it is utterly unreasonable to pick and choose what they will admit and what they will reject, solely on the ground that the former supports and the latter destroys their pet theory of his perfection. It would be just as irrational in me were I to pick out all the bad things and sayings ascribed to Christ, to ground upon *them* an opinion of him that he never said or did anything good and true; and, then, when confronted with really good and true sayings ascribed to him, I should turn round and say I do not believe he ever said them, because they upset my theory that he was wholly bad. I do not think my worst enemy would charge me with having ever done that or anything like it.

---

* See Lecture V. of this Series.

But now let us review the situation. There is the orthodox Christian world claiming that Jesus Christ was not only perfect man, but perfect God also. And there are the Unitarians aiding and abetting the orthodox and even putting weapons of offence in their hands by declaring that Jesus was a perfect man and far better and wiser than any other religious teacher the world ever had. The consequence of the elevation of Jesus to the level of Deity has been to place him really above the One Living and True God. Even if he were a real God, he would still be a successful rival of God and a supplanter of God in the affections of men. In spite of all Athanasian assertions and contradictions, there would still be two Gods—one who became man and the other who did not; one God who intercedes with the other God on man's behalf; one God who, being the Saviour from the wrath of the other God, deserves and wins man's greater love and closer allegiance. And we not only see the dire results of this mythology in the past history and present conditions of Christendom, but it is brought home to some of us by a most bitter and painful experience that to love God best and not to love Christ best will surely receive the penalty of as much cruelty as modern civilisation will permit. There are present in this Church at this moment persons of the highest moral character, of exceptional amiability and sweetness of disposition, who have within a few weeks past been driven out of comfortable homes and had to seek shelter elsewhere—all in the name of Christ, for Christ's honour and glory—because they love God best and do not worship Christ or call themselves after his name. In hundreds of ways we find strife and division and the marring of domestic peace and love entirely caused by the love of Christ and the cruel demands made by the words ascribed to him in the Gospels:—"He that loveth father or mother, son or daughter, more than me is not worthy of me." If more instances were wanted I could go on adding to the list for hours and days and then not exhaust the terrible indictment. Wherever the spirit of Christianity survives in its fulness there is the enemy of justice, of charity and of true brotherly and family love.

<small>Matt. x. 37.</small>

And from all this and much more, I infer that for every one of us, whether we are Christians, Unitarians, or Theists, nay, even also for Jews and for all non-Christians who have to live under so-called Christian governments—I say, for every one of us this question of what Jesus Christ really was, what he really said and taught, is the most important practical question to which our earnest attention could be called.

I wish and even heartily pray that before I die I may know all that is to be known on this great theme; that I may not be blinded by prejudices, however strong, however dear; that I may not be biassed by any hopes, however exalted; that my judgment may not be warped even by my highest religious instincts; but that I may believe about

Jesus Christ exactly what God wishes me to believe and exactly what is the truth: and although the real Jesus has gone far enough away from touch of our praise or blame, I pray that I may not be unfair to him in any word or thought, but think and speak only what is just and true. To this great end, I ask you to follow me in my search with patience, caution and sympathy. With patience when I may hurt your sensibilities, with caution when I may seem to you too intrepid, and with sympathy when the difficulties and puzzles of the task are too great for my unravelling.

I earnestly hope that these Lectures on Jesus Christ will draw the attention of the honest folk among orthodox Bishops, Clergy, and Nonconformist ministers to the steadfast examination of that book called *The Four Gospels as Historical Records*, which its very learned author has sent forth anonymously with the one sole aim of getting the undivided, undistracted attention of scholars like himself to the actual statements of his book, to its elaborate arguments and startling conclusions. Intelligent artizans who read it will know what to think and to say of those of their clergy who deem it prudent to ignore it. A rude and inevitable judgment must overtake at last those professed teachers on whom the mighty responsibility of knowledge has fallen, and who yet lack the love of truth or the moral courage to set that knowledge openly before those whom they are sent to teach and to enlighten. I have the author's permission to quote here his own words from a letter to a distinguished Churchman in reference to his book on the Four Gospels :—

> I have shown that in the Four Gospels there is, in strictness of speech, no history at all, and that many of the most momentous incidents in these narratives (as, *e.g.*, the whole Judas story from beginning to end) are mere fictions. Are not you bound, not merely to assert, but to show that I am wrong? If you decline to do this, will not your failure or refusal give countenance to the horrible suspicion that the English clergy and the English people are content to uphold, and to profess faith in a system which they know rests on a false foundation, and that this falsehood is to be maintained at all costs?

The book on the Four Gospels deals, however, with a subject not to be confounded with my present one. I believe that book to be of value fully equal to the high importance of the topic of which it treats—viz., the unhistorical and untrustworthy character of the Four Gospels. My work is a wholly different one. It is addressed to those who have hardly begun to suspect that their Gospels are untrue in any point. It is addressed to those who read and value their Gospels, who read them blindfold and think that the Evangelists are desscribing a perfect God who was also a perfect man. I am only going to ask them to look with me, and with as much honesty and intelligence as they can bring into the quest, at the pictures presented to us of Jesus Christ by his so-called friends. I must assume the general accuracy of all the pictures; I must assume the equal probability of Jesus having said the true things and the untrue things, the good things and the bad things attributed to him;

excepting only, as in the two cases I have pointed out, those sayings which are too bad to impute to any human being. And on these assumptions—which I do not create for myself but simply borrow from the Christians to whom these Lectures are addressed, and to whom the Gospels are more than accurate, the inspired words of the Holy Ghost—I will endeavour to draw correct inferences concerning the Christ therein depicted. When my occupation with them is completed, I must turn to the controversy with the Unitarians, who will require a somewhat different line of argument.

But I say once more, that my object in going over the whole ground is not to repeat unpalatable conclusions, but to make my own steps more sure in the path of truth and fact: to learn all I can of what I do not know, and to unlearn any errors into which I may have fallen. In thus clearing and sharpening my own perception of truth, I hope earnestly that I may help others to do the same. And once recognising the fact that the chief hindrance, if not the only hindrance, to the more rapid spread of the knowledge and love of God throughout Christendom is due to the false position now occupied by Jesus Christ, we may rest assured that, next to the supreme duties of having our own hearts right with God and full of justice and love towards our fellow-men, no duty is so urgent upon us as the endeavour to destroy the foundations of that idolatry and priestcraft which are working such cruel mischief in these times. Properly read and duly examined, the Four Gospels seem to me to furnish weapons of attack against the idolatry of Christ and morbid sentiment about him which are absolutely irresistible. "Let us not be weary in well-doing, for in due season we shall reap if we faint not."

Lecture II.

It is my desire to deal with the subject of these lectures with due solemnity; not to allow myself to forget that to the large majority of my countrymen the name of Christ is as the name of God, and that many, who call themselves Christians and who at the same time deny the Godhead of Jesus, regard him as occupying a very lofty place of superhuman dignity. But while, on every ground, some regard is due to the religious feelings of others, a far higher regard is due to Truth. While we would not willingly shock tender sensibilities, nor outrage pious sentiment, we must not shrink from the infliction of a temporary pain which we firmly believe will conduce to higher and lasting happiness. The world, and especially that part of it which is called "The Religious World," has suffered much, but never more than at this moment, from unworthy equivocations, from cowardly evasions, and from studied silences. Hundreds of excellent people, clergymen and ministers of all denominations, continue to use phrases, which already possess a definite popular value, in a private sense of their own; and the result is that they leave their congregations under the false impression that they and the preacher think exactly alike. If the preacher really believes that this kind of teaching can advance his hearers one step, he is utterly mistaken. If he thinks he is preserving the worn-out coin by putting a new stamp of his own upon it, he will be doing his best to encourage false weights and measures, and unconsciously depraving the intellectual honesty of those who listen to him.

Not in this way must we deal with the greatest theological question of the day. We must have no mental reservations, no pious frauds, not the very shadow of equivocation. Even if we are wrong and Christendom is right, our great plainness of speech will enable the orthodox the more easily to refute our errors; while those who listen to us will never be able to reproach us with the concealment or the disguise of our real opinions.

In this Lecture I must endeavour to deal more in detail with the sources of our knowledge of Christ than I was able to do in my Introductory Lecture.

The sole sources of our knowledge of Christ are the New Testament, and Tradition. The former, a collection of writings purporting to give us the history of Jesus, and some of the sayings and doings of himself and of his early followers. The latter—Tradition—being embodied in the creeds and customs of the organised society called the Church, which professes to have been established by Jesus himself, to have gathered all its doctrine, rites and ceremonies from the same authority; and to be, at this day and hour, under the supernatural guidance and teaching of the glorified and deified Jesus Christ.

These two authorities, viz., the New Testament and the Church, are, as everyone knows, held in different estimation as authorities by different sections of Christendom. Some put the New Testament before the Church, others put the Church before the New Testament. But both are agreed in admitting that without either the one or the other, we should have known nothing whatever of Jesus Christ.

We *must* remember this. It is an important fact. No claim is now set up that we know of Jesus, as we know of God, by intuition or by our natural reason. No one has ever been so bold or so stupid as to say that a belief in Jesus as God is part of Natural religion. On the contrary, this entire absence of Christ from the conclusions of Natural Theology, and this utter incongruity of an incarnate God with the natural religious sentiments in their highest development, have been dwelt upon by the advocates of Revealed Religion as among its greatest recommendations. Believers in Revelation point with pride to the fact that, on this great central belief in the God-man, Nature and the human heart are absolutely silent, or when they speak they are hostile to it. "How would you ever have known?" they ask triumphantly, "How would you ever have known that a God came down from Heaven to save a ruined world, without the agency of the New Testament or of the Church to reveal the tidings?" Nothing can be more satisfactory to Theists than the admission which is thus made. It saves endless controversy about "adaptation to man's needs" and so forth, and brings us close to the point at issue. Is the New Testament, or is the Church, or are neither of them, to be depended upon for strict accuracy in their respective accounts of what Jesus was, of what he did, and of what he said?

To answer first as regards the Church. Which of all the Churches do you mean, from the primitive Church which was never united in belief, downwards to the Swedenborgian Church of the New Jerusalem? Is it Eastern or Western, Episcopalian or Presbyterian?—So on, we might ask, through the three hundred sections of Christendom. Suppose that we have at last found the true Church, established by Jesus, and that her credentials are beyond suspicion. How much can this Church tell us about Jesus Christ that we are bound to believe without question? They will begin by saying that he was God, that he was born without a human father, that he wrought miracles, rose again from the dead, and with his human body, with flesh, bones and all things appertaining to the completeness of man's nature, ascended into Heaven and is now sitting on a throne at the right hand of God. Well, all this, we say, may be true, though it appears very unlikely; but how do you guarantee the truth of any one of your statements? I am quite willing to believe everything on sufficient evidence. I only want to be furnished with the proofs of all these wonderful things. The Church answers—"All these things were believed and duly attested by the earliest followers and most intimate companions of Jesus, who handed them down through their early converts, through their bishops and elders, generation after generation, unchanged till they have reached us." But again, supposing that you have received in this manner exactly what the companions of Jesus believed and no more, how do you know that they were not mistaken? "Oh!" says the Church, "they could not have been mistaken, they led such holy lives, and died as witnesses for the truth of what they affirmed." But, if my memory does not fail me, many men who have led holy lives have been miserably deluded in some of their opinions; martyrs by the hundred can be brought forward who died in defence of exactly opposite and contradictory beliefs. Hostile Churches took it in turns to kill and be killed. So the holiness of life goes for very little, and the proof of infallibility from martyrdom goes for nothing at all. Your assertion, then, of the absolute credibility of the earliest followers of Jesus is of no more weight as evidence than your assertion that Jesus went up bodily into the sky. If you go on to affirm that the case was exceptional, and that Jesus being God infallibly inspired his Apostles to say that he was God, you are only arguing in a circle and we end where we began—without reasonable proof of one of your assertions.

The arguments drawn from the honesty of the Apostles is, I believe, exploded, as only the most ill-informed and foolish of dogmatists will venture to say that, if Jesus and the Apostles were not all that they are represented to be, therefore they were rogues and impostors. The disrespect of this assumption, unwarranted as it is, is only surpassed by its ignorance. As a matter of fact, it has been recently repeated by Christian advocates.

But the Church will go on to say, " Look at my wonderful and rapid growth, and my conquest of paganism ; my triumphs over barbarism, my fruits of civilisation." To this one can only reply that were the triumphs of Christendom one hundred-fold more than they have been, were there no dark corners in the Church's house, no blood-stains on her once cruel hands, no dying yells of outraged Jew and murdered Indian mingling with her jubilee, no stone of stumbling nor rock of offence in her feeble obstructions to the progress of Science, no breath of hatred, malice and all uncharitableness in her toothless maledictions ; still all her finest achievements and purest virtues could never bear witness as to a matter of historical fact, could never supply even presumptive evidence for that which can only be attested independently of herself. The painter might as well try to prove that one of his remote ancestry excelled in the art of music by the mere exhibition of his own latest masterpiece. There is no logical connection whatever between the claims made by or for Jesus and the very highest achievements of the Church.

Moreover—though it is a branch of our enquiry which we cannot now follow—the pretensions of the Church can be matched over and over again in the histories of the rise and progress of other great religions in the world besides Christianity. If the argument from success be admitted at all, it only proves too much. So far then as the Church or Churches of Christendom are to be trusted, we can get no evidence from them worthy of the name sufficiently trustworthy to be depended upon for an accurate account of the nature and history of Jesus Christ. For evidence, we get only assumptions.

And a great deal of this that I have said respecting the Church applies equally to those who present the New Testament to us on false pretences, *i.e.*, as a Divine and infallible record of actual facts. But the New Testament itself must be considered on its own grounds. With the sole exception of the Book of Revelation, which condemns itself by its own bad temper and anathemas, not one of the New Testament books makes any claim of Divine origin. The author of the Third Gospel and of the Acts of the Apostles expressly affirms the human sources from which he obtained his information. While the Fourth Gospel is supplemented by a verse from a hand not that of the disciple, John himself: "This is the disciple which testifieth of these things and we (*i.e.*, the writer, and others) know that his testimony is true." [John xxi. 24.]

This is the most decided expression which I can remember to occur in all the Gospels and Acts of the Apostles approaching to a claim even for accuracy, but still this is not worth the paper that it is written on. There is not the shadow of a shade of a claim that the writings are infallibly true, or that they were written under Divine inspiration. I think this fact in itself furnishes an additional reason why we should give to the quasi-historical parts of the New Testament due consideration. At least, they do not insult our understandings by any preposterous claim. When, or by whom, they were written, no one can possibly tell with certainty. All that is certainly known is that the oldest copies of them which are now in existence were made not earlier than 300 years after the events which they profess to record. These copies may, or may not, be faithful: may, or may not, have tallied with the originals which are now lost. At all events we cannot go further back for evidence than that late date; for although some early writers may contain quotations, or what seem to be quotations of words out of our oldest MSS., this fact would not guarantee that the whole of the rest of the books from which they quoted stands correctly copied in our MSS. It would only give a little weight to a probability, and that is all. The external evidence then for the literal accuracy of the New Testament records is next to nothing, and we are therefore driven to weigh the historical claims of the books from a consideration of their contents. What internal evidence, then, do we find that the writers of the first five books of the New Testament are giving us authentic and trustworthy history?

To answer this important question, several essays have been already written, and the subject is hardly yet exhausted. But by far the most important and the strongest of them all is the book recently published by Messrs. Williams and Norgate, entitled, *The Four Gospels as Historical Records,* which begins by proving that the book of the Acts of the Apostles is hopelessly contradictory of the only Epistles of St. Paul which are accounted now as really written by him. It would carry us too far away from our main line to examine minutely the books of the New Testament referred to. Suffice it to say, as a summing up of the careful analysis and criticism of learned men, that these New Testament narratives may have some basis of fact, *e.g.*: that there probably was such a person as Jesus of Nazareth, and that his life was, according to the standard of those times, extremely pure and beneficent, that he made himself obnoxious to the Jewish authorities, who secured his condemnation by the Roman Governor on the accusation that he was dangerous to the Empire.

These bald outlines are common to all the books, and may fairly be trusted as highly probable. But beyond that a careful reader will observe endless contradictions and discrepancies of such a nature as to exclude the idea that the writers were sufficiently acquainted with the ordinary facts of the life of Jesus to justify the use of the term *historical* in speaking of their conflicting accounts. In other words, they cannot all be true at the same time, and we have no certain way of discovering which writer speaks the truth, when two or more of them give contradictory accounts of the same event. Now if their writings only set forth events such as are commonly or even rarely occurring amongst ourselves, but at all events, actually occurring, we should even then be compelled to distrust their accuracy; but when, in addition to such ordinary matters as whether Jesus was crucified on a Friday or on a Thursday, whether the genealogies of Christ's lineage from David in Matthew and in Luke can be reconciled with each other, or either of them with Old Testament records; when, besides all such things, we have to accept tales of magic and miracle utterly foreign to general human experience and in some cases purposely puerile, we are impelled by the very constitution of our own minds to distrust the books a hundred times more than ever, and to doubt almost whether there be a grain of fact at the bottom of so much palpable fiction.

But I use the word "fiction" not in a sense derogatory of the honour of the writers. That these books were *not* written by men who knew Jesus personally cannot be doubted, and therefore they wrote from second hand, aye, third and fourth hand, if you like, no one knows how long after Jesus and His followers had been dead and buried. But whoever wrote them may have written honestly what had been told them, what had become the floating and perpetually growing legendary traditions about a very remarkable and remarkably kind and good man. What would not one give for a Peter, a James, or a John to come back and tell us the simple life of Christ as he saw it and understood it? But we possess not one single fragment of writing upon which we can lay our hands and say with absolute confidence—*this* at least is a perfectly true and uncorrupted statement of some part of the history or sayings of Jesus, written by one who knew, and saw, and heard him, who was not under any delusion at the time, and who wrote in perfect good faith. You will perceive then that the only sources of our knowledge of Christ are untrustworthy, deeply, hopelessly untrustworthy, and that we are driven to almost mere guessing to form any conception of him at all.

In attempting to answer the question, "What think ye of Christ?" it is necessary to show first of all that almost whatever we think of Christ is equally without historical foundation, that we have no evidence, worthy of the name, to support the Church's claim as to his nature, his character, his deeds and his sayings. Probability more or less strong is all we can attain unto on this point. Now I say deliberately and earnestly to the Christians that *this absolutely unhistorical character* of both their Church Traditions and New Testament scriptures proves at once that Jesus was not Almighty God. For had he been really God, he could not, without doing a great wrong, have left it so difficult to discover the truth and fact about himself. As the case stands, he took not the very least pains to substantiate even the most important statements concerning matters of fact, he left not a scrap of writing for us to read, and left no rule whatever whereby we might be guided as to what he said and what he did not say.

Nor will it avail anything to appeal to the permanence of Christianity in proof of the truth of the Gospels. Brahmanism was almost driven out of India by Buddhism, 600 years or so before Christ, but Brahmanism recovered from the shock, drove Buddha beyond her walls, and resumed the primæval sway, and has a history at least 4,000 years old. Buddhism in turn has conquered Eastern Asia, and with 400,000,000 of believers bids defiance to the waves of Christianity which break in ripples on her wide-spread shore. Mahomedanism too, beaten back from Western Europe by the monogamy of northern races, drove Christianity altogether out of the provinces of Asia Minor and the North of Africa, and has won vast populations in India before whom Christianity kneels in vain.

It only remains for me to say that it was absolutely necessary to clear the ground for the proper consideration of our thoughts about Christ. It is true beyond question that no absolute reliance can be placed either on the teachings of the Church, or on the New Testament narratives; but it is equally true that a man of great goodness of purpose, and possessing the very genius of true religion, lived and died in Judæa about eighteen centuries ago; that his life and death exercised, and still exercise, a vast power over millions of men and women, both for good and for evil; that in spite of the exaggerations of an almost pardonable idolatry, in spite also of the clouds of incredible myth in which his biography has been shrouded, there still remains a residuum of substantial fact, and a valuable, though perhaps not original contribution to the religious and moral principles of mankind, which only a bigoted scepticism would ignore, and which, as devout Theists, we are as much bound to recognise and to use, as we are bound to reject and denounce the falsehood and superstition which have been mixed up with the sober truth.

A discourse like this is, in my opinion, like offering a stone to one who wants bread; yet sometimes stones are wanted quite as much as bread, and even more. Now and then such discourses are absolutely necessary, and I trust that the present Lecture will not have been altogether without spiritual nourishment, if it should lead a single doubting or enquiring heart to the Father's footstool with this petition: "Lead me in Thy truth, and teach me; Be Thou also my guide, and lead me for Thy name's sake."

Lecture III.

It will be remembered that, in our search for fact and truth about Jesus Christ, the plan I laid down was first to enter into the controversy with orthodox Christians who believe that Jesus was a God on earth; and for this purpose I should have to assume the accuracy of the records of his words and deeds, my conviction being strong that there is no better weapon wherewith to attack that orthodox belief than the very words of the Four Gospels. The Church never took a wiser step to uphold her dogmas than when she prohibited the people at large from reading the New Testament. For no sooner did Luther and Erasmus throw open this book so that all might read and judge for themselves, than it began to undermine belief in the dogmas and to impair the authority of the Church itself. This process of disintegration has been going on with increasing force ever since; and no dogma of the Church is now in greater peril than that of the Deity of Christ, on which her whole authority depends.

In looking once more through the Four Gospels, it becomes manifest that the group of sayings attributed to Christ which are commonly called the *Sermon on the Mount* contains the most convincing proofs against the idea that he claimed to be God. And although I unhesitatingly admit that in other parts of the New Testament, and especially in the Fourth Gospel, words are ascribed to him which cannot be made to harmonise with the *Sermon on the Mount*, this very contradiction helps to overthrow the authority of the New Testament in establishing any doctrine concerning Christ at all; and helps, therefore, to undermine the authority of the Church, which she is always claiming to rest upon words of Christ in the Gospels. I need hardly repeat to you that there is no just ground for believing that the Sermon on the Mount was delivered just as it stands, but only for regarding it as a mere collection of sayings bearing a common theological resemblance, and all in the same tone which belongs to that earlier period in the life of Jesus when he was an unsophisticated Jew and a simple teacher of morals and religion. And in this light, the Sermon on the Mount has a most important bearing on our present enquiry. There will be no need to quote it *verbatim*, as I shall give the references to certain passages which I may have to cite.

The Sermon divides itself with tolerable clearness into the subjects of morals and religion, though they overlap, of course, and by their very nature they are hardly separable. The religious portion we will examine first, in order to show what is the only Theology that can legitimately be drawn from it. From first to last Jesus Christ speaks of only one

God, whom he calls very frequently "our Father" and "your Father which is in heaven." And although he uses language asserting his own authority, which jars upon our sense of humility (*e.g.*, when he sets his own authority above that of the Decalogue, and alludes to himself as the Judge of men at the last day), never once does he venture near the impiety of placing himself on a level with God; never once does he speak of himself as a Saviour, or Mediator; never once does he allude even faintly to the doctrine of the Atonement, or lead us to regard himself as anything more than a teacher commissioned or even self-appointed to enlighten men as to their duty and to elevate their spiritual conceptions of it so as to affect not only their conduct but their character. Whether or not the Scribes and Pharisees of his day deserved his reproaches, there can be no hesitation in admiring the spirit of his words: "Except your righteousness shall exceed the righteousness of the Scribes and Pharisees, ye shall in no wise enter into the kingdom of heaven." Formalism and punctilious regard for religious rites and ceremonies have ever been, and perhaps always will be, hindrances to true spiritual religion and to real righteousness of heart, while they have fostered the vices of pride and bigotry. But it is when we come to the subject of prayer that we find the teaching of Christ in deadly opposition to the whole Christian scheme. In the plainest possible language he teaches his disciples to pray "Our Father which art in heaven," without

<small>Matt. v. 20.</small>

<small>Matt. vi. 9.</small>

a word of intercession or reference to himself as a mediator; their first petition is to be: "Hallowed be Thy Name," the third "Thy will be done"; and when the prayer for forgiveness comes, it is based not on any atoning blood, but on the condition of our having forgiven our debtors. No sooner is the form of prayer ended than he re-emphasises this condition in these words: "For if ye forgive men their trespasses, your heavenly Father will also forgive you; but if ye forgive not men their trespasses, neither will your Father forgive your trespasses." I say to the whole of orthodox Christendom that no words of mine could more completely make an end of your Christian scheme of salvation and atonement and forgiveness than these words of your own Lord Jesus Christ. And in teaching men to pray to their Father in heaven and to cast all their cares upon Him, it was deemed by Christ quite enough to understand and remember that holy name of Father which gives every child of His a perfect right to go to Him with every thought and wish and fear. And as if some of his hearers might be still so dense as not to see the full meaning of that blessed name and all that it implies, Jesus still further adds: "If ye then, being evil, know how to give good gifts unto your children, how much more shall your Father which is in heaven give good things unto them that ask Him?" Thus, exactly as the Theist does, Christ argued upwards to God, our heavenly Father, from the human love which we men and women feel for our own children.

<small>Matt. vi. 14, 15.</small>

<small>Matt. vii. 11.</small>

The pity of it is that Christ ever said or is reported to have said anything to mar the truth and simplicity of this prayer, *e.g.*, that we should ask God for what we want in his (Jesus') name and for his sake. Of course I still think that some of the ideas concerning prayer which Jesus held and taught were quite wrong. We have a right to pray to God for anything we want; but we have no right to dictate to our Father what He shall do, and no right to expect that He will ever give us anything which He sees fit to withhold. *E.g.*, "Ask and it shall be given you; seek and ye shall find; knock and it shall be opened unto you; for everyone that asketh receiveth, and he that seeketh findeth, and to him that knocketh it shall be opened." This is simply untrue and misleading. No greater calamity could befall us than to be thus able, by prayer, to get our own way. I must also in fairness point out that even in this Sermon on the Mount, the beautiful theology concerning the Fatherly Love of God already quoted is deeply marred by threats of Hell-fire. I must also remind you that the very words of the Lord's Prayer, at least the first half of them, had been in use in the Jewish Synagogues fifty years before he was born. This in no way detracts from the value of the Prayer, or from the truth and beauty of its conception of God: it only proves that, at that period of his life, Jesus was an unperverted Jew.

Jesus is reported to have said something else calculated to disturb the serene complacency of

[margin: John xiv. 13, 14.]
[margin: Matt. vi. 7, 8.]

orthodoxy in the following words, "Not every one that saith unto me, Lord, Lord, shall enter into the kingdom of heaven, but he that doeth the will of my Father which is in heaven." On another occasion he said, "If thou wilt enter into life, keep the commandments." How do the Sacerdotalists reconcile these words with their insistence on the Sacraments and on belief in Christ's Godhead, as the only means of entering into life eternal? I do not envy them their dilemma; for they believe that Jesus Christ gave these rules of salvation and also at another time quite opposite rules, and was still Almighty God even when he contradicted himself. When he said, "Keep the commandments" he was understood to mean the Decalogue. And what possible harmony can be established between that condition of entering eternal life and such words as these: "He that believeth and is baptised shall be saved; and he that believeth not shall be damned"?* Only in the fifteenth chapter of Luke and in the parable of the Prodigal Son, and of the Publican and the Pharisee, do we find that higher and sweeter teaching of fatherly love and forgiveness. Most of the parables are hopelessly at variance with it, and are full of awful threatenings. The allusions to hell-fire in the Sermon on the Mount must not pass without observing that, in the days of Christ, no one had even a dream that the torments of hell

<small>Matt. vii. 21.</small>
<small>Matt. xix. 17.</small>
<small>Mark xvi. 16.</small>

---

* I am aware that these words are now regarded as spurious. But no law has yet been passed to prohibit them from being read in churches and schools as the words of Christ.

would be terminable. Christ's own story of the Rich Man and Lazarus, with the great and impassable gulf between them, was only a faithful reproduction of the ideas common at that time, and which had been imbibed by the Jews during the Babylonish captivity, and were only abandoned by them after the dispersion which followed the destruction of Jerusalem. But every form of the doctrine of hell, which implies a need of deliverance and escape from it, is so much downright denial of the real Fatherhood of God. No doubt there is a hell awaiting every one of us who needs God's cleansing fires; but it is a hell which only leads to heaven, and is not separated from eternal blessedness by any great gulf fixed; it is a hell which, for our very salvation, we cannot afford to evade or to be bought-off from by any precious blood. The hell of the Sermon on the Mount, though not obtrusive, is still a grave blot on teaching which is otherwise true and good.

It is important for those who believe in the Godhead of Christ to notice the almost contemptuous tone in which he speaks of portions of the Decalogue, *e.g.*, "Ye have heard that it was said by them of old time, Thou shalt not kill," etc. Now, it is inconceivable that if Jesus was Almighty God, he could speak so scornfully of those commandments which he, as a member of the Trinity, had himself written on the Tables of Stone on Mount Sinai. Moreover, after saying that " till heaven and earth pass, one jot or one tittle of the law shall in nowise pass from the law till all be fulfilled," he goes on to condemn the law of divorce and the law concerning oaths, etc., thus openly contradicting himself.

_{Matt. v. 31-37.}

But now we must turn to the moral teaching of this Sermon. I will begin by enumerating some of its good features.

Jesus Christ herein goes to the root of the whole matter, laying siege to the heart rather than to the hands, insisting upon our keeping the spirit of the law rather than the letter of it. And in this feature he shines out strongly as a true lover of God and lover of righteousness. Purity of heart with him is everything; his best promise is kept for that when he says, "Blessed are the pure in heart, for they shall see God." And for all who feel their sinfulness and weakness, he says, "Blessed are they that do hunger and thirst after righteousness, for they shall be filled." You cannot find, I think, anywhere a more perfect specimen of what I call religious morality than in these two Beatitudes. I admire them with unqualified satisfaction and pleasure. His expansion of some commandments of the Decalogue, though not rising to that high level, is yet worthy of our commendation, for he shows that the feelings of our hearts towards each other are far more important than our conduct, because it is from the feelings that the conduct springs. In all this he stands high indeed as a moral teacher, and when he bids us actually to love our enemies and return good for evil, that we may be truly and deservedly the children of our Father

Matt. v. 44, 45.

in heaven, he touches the highest standard of which we have heard. I do not pretend here to advocate the literal performance of his precepts of non-resistance. I have dealt with this large subject already in previous sermons. But I say that if we do earnestly desire to be worthy children of God, and to be like Him, we must adopt and cultivate more and more this spirit of non-resistance and non-retaliation, and not trample it in the dust, after the manner of the mass of civilised Christians. His precepts about almsgiving, and fasting, and the saying of prayers in public, are all in the same high tone, inculcating deep sincerity of heart and the absolute avoidance of vanity and ostentation. No less valuable is his teaching in regard to earthly treasure and the love of money. Money is either our servant or our master. If we let it master us, away will go the mastership of God. "Ye cannot Matt. vi. 24. serve God and Mammon." Again we must admire his severe rebuke of the judging and censorious spirit which is so frequently forgotten or despised by the Christian world. It is almost the last thing we do when anyone injures or offends us, to try to put ourselves in his place and think kindly of him, to judge him mercifully and to find excuses for him. But this is exactly what Jesus bids us do. And we have already seen that here, as indeed also elsewhere, Jesus insists on our full and free forgiveness of trespasses against ourselves, even after Matt. xviii. 22. four hundred and ninety repetitions of the offence in one day. This may be Eastern hyperbole, but it is magnificent for all that, and ought to put to eternal shame our brutal resentment and our dogged sulkiness.

But in spite of all this superb morality we cannot shut our eyes to certain and ineffaceable moral blemishes in it. I mention first the painful prominence which Jesus gives throughout his discourse to the hope of reward or to the fear of punishment. There are only three striking exceptions: "Blessed are the pure in heart, for they shall see God;" "Blessed are they that do hunger and thirst after righteousness, for they shall be filled;" and "Love your enemies, so that ye may be like your Father which is in heaven." Some captious persons might say that even these are held out as bribes, but that objection is withered with scorn by our own Conscience, which tells us that the seeing of God, the being filled with righteousness and being worthy of true sonship to God—no matter what you call them, rewards or consequences—are certainly privileges which we ought to desire with all our hearts, and fix our strongest hopes on attaining. Not one word can fairly be said against those three passages. But the very grounds on which we admire them compel us to object strongly to the oft-repeated words of Jesus, that God will reward us openly, *i.e.*, by some outward and visible mark of approval, for doing what is right. All the Beatitudes, except those two I have named, have attached to them a promise of some mundane or personal reward. He could not well help it, for it

Matt. vi. 1.

was the atmosphere in which he was born and lived and taught. To be sharers in the kingdom of heaven (certainly understood to be here on earth, though this does not affect the bribe), to inherit the earth, to be *called* the Children of God (*i.e.*, to have men's praise), to be greatest in the kingdom of heaven, to escape the casting into hell, to be reminded that there is no reward for loving them that love us, to be promised that if we do our alms in secret our Father will reward us openly, to be offered the same reward for secret prayer and for disguised fasting, to be induced to forgive each other in order that we ourselves should be forgiven, to be told to lay up treasure where thief and moth cannot enter, to be told to seek first the Kingdom of God and His righteousness, and then all other things, such as food and drink and clothing, shall be added unto us, to avoid cruel and unkind judgment of others only lest we should ourselves be judged harshly, and finally, to keep the good precepts of Christ that we may not be in danger of final destruction—all these are moral blemishes upon a picture of great moral sublimity, and must, if we appreciate what is best and highest in it, lead us, if not to condemn, to modify greatly our estimate of the teacher.

Now, to my Christian friends I would say a few words as gently as I can put them. Your Lord Jesus Christ in this Sermon of his openly states his own belief in Devils and Hell-fire—both of which, when carefully examined, are detractions from the infinite justice and love of our Heavenly Father. These alone would be sufficient to prove to me that Jesus was not Almighty God, but had fallen into the errors and superstitions current in his day. Yet I will make you a present of these, for the sake of argument, and on the plea that they may be regarded as matters of pure speculation. Let us leave them out of our estimate of Jesus Christ, and take only the blemishes which I have pointed out in the moral part, and that ineffaceable blot which appears so often in the promise of reward—open, temporal, mundane or eternal—for doing what is right. Can you honestly say that you believe Jesus Christ to have been God Almighty upon earth, if he said things and urged motives for conduct which you and I must feel to be wrong, unworthy of man at his highest state? For in so far as those promises of reward were caught at and embraced, they were inimical to true virtue, and turned obedience into supreme selfishness. If we are forced, as it seems to me we are forced, to admit the moral blemishes when they are pointed out in this, by far the best and noblest and sweetest collection of the sayings of Jesus Christ, what will be felt by us when we turn over the pages and scarcely find an echo of this grand teaching all through the rest of the Gospels. For you and for me there is no middle course. Jesus Christ either was, or was not, the Incarnate God; either knew, or did not know, the true constituents of true virtue; gave us, or did not give us, the highest motives for conduct and character and none other. If you and I can criticise him, if you and I are compelled to criticise him on moral grounds, I ask where can you find proof of his Godhead to nullify our adverse criticism ? By the side of such a question all literary criticism of the Gospels fades into utter insignificance.

Lecture IV.

"*And Jesus went about all the cities and villages . . . . healing every sickness and every disease among the people.*"
MATTHEW ix. 35.

"*And when he had called unto him his twelve disciples, he gave them power against unclean spirits, and to heal all manner of sickness and all manner of disease.*"
MATTHEW x. 1.

"*Heal the sick, cleanse the lepers, raise the dead, cast out devils; freely ye have received, freely give.*"
MATTHEW x. 8.

WE are all, I trust, humane enough to be more or less charmed with that part of the life of Christ which tells us of his sympathy with human suffering and of his readiness to come to its relief. Our hearts respond to the cries for pity and help from the lame, the halt and the blind, from the outcast woman of Syro-Phœnicia, from the lips of nobleman and centurion pleading for the life of child and servant. And we read with a healthy glow of satisfaction how the hand of mercy was outstretched to them, how one and all had their burdens lifted off their weary hearts, how the eyes of the blind were opened, the tongue of the dumb was loosed and the deaf were made to hear; how the dying were rescued, and how even the very dead were raised, and the broken-hearted widow was made to rejoice over the restoration of her only son as he was being carried to the tomb. We love to linger over the cleansing of the lepers, the leaping of the lame and the crippled, and the release of disordered minds from the terrible bondage of insanity. Just as we weep with them that weep, so do we rejoice with them whom the Christ made to rejoice. And although it has been falsely asserted that these acts of healing mercy came into the world for the first time in the towns of Judæa and Galilee when Jesus went about doing good and healing all manner of disease among the people; although, on the contrary, in other parts of the world and even in the remote civilisation of ancient Egypt the sick and the needy were often lovingly tended and cared for, we nevertheless admit that the record of this healing part of Christ's work gave an enormous stimulus to the sympathies of men, and kindled in many cold hearts the flame of a Divine love and compassion. Not for worlds, then, would I allow anything I may utter to-day to weaken our native pity for the sufferings of mankind or to weaken the effect of the noble examples of those who have done what they could to relieve them.

Now, it has pleased God of His great and stupendous love to us men to permit us to be the subjects of pain and disease. Almost to every one in turn comes the bitter experience and to many it is a life-long burden. His great and gracious rule has been hitherto in all the ages to let these agencies of pain and disease work out the grand purposes of redeeming and raising our race from a state of mere animal or vegetable existence into a high, social, moral, and spiritual life. To-day, I cannot recapitulate the arguments by which this is absolutely proved. I simply take it for granted that every one who has given due thought to the subject will confess at once that we owe all our moral and spiritual elevation to those very agencies of pain and sorrow which we are compelled to wrestle with and to overcome. But, when once this is clearly seen, we see also the reason why God should leave us to ourselves, to the exercise of the natural faculties which He has given, to the combined influences of necessity and of duty which in time would work out the high moral purpose of suffering, and at length, when that purpose was fully accomplished, should issue, as it probably will, in the extinction of pain and disease altogether. Everything is tending that way now and has been for long ages, only the progress has been greatly accelerated in these later times.

Specially must we notice that the healing of diseases can only be acquired by the most laborious and difficult processes of education and training. In ancient times, only the fewest and rarest of our race could qualify themselves for this great task; and to-day by common consent our medical students are obliged to devote much longer time to the completion of their studies than students of any other branch of knowledge or art. In fact, the true healer has never done learning his art. It is a lifelong research, involving ever fresh duties of observation and reflection, and the perpetual correction of previous, and perhaps popular, errors. I have called your attention to this, not only to the lasting credit of the medical profession, but especially to mark it as a feature of God's unbroken order in the world, that not only pain and disease should be here, but that the whole process of healing should be difficult and laborious, and the art acquired only by those who by faithful diligence have become worthy to attain it. This is God's obvious rule, and any departure from it demands explanation and moral justification.

The miracles of healing recorded in the New Testament are an obvious departure from the Divine Order, and they ought not to be accepted by us as true history without ample evidence of the strongest kind, or without enquiry into the object for which the departure was made. Now, as to the evidence that they occurred, we need not waste any time in shewing that we have no evidence whatever that would satisfy us in support of any ordinary event, and therefore no extraordinary event could be established on such feeble testimony. It should never be forgotten that the Four Gospels have not the remotest claim to be regarded as History. Nevertheless, as some so-called miracles of healing or Faith-cures have undoubtedly been performed in all ages of the world and have been recently exhibited in our own country and on the continent, it is only reasonable to say that, though the miracles of Christ are not properly attested, yet some of them, viz., some of what are called Faith-cures might well have happened. This admission, however, will not include the raising of the dead or any other recorded miracle which could not be brought into the proper category of Faith-cures.

But let us now admit, for the sake of argument, that all the recorded miracles really occurred; the great question we have to ask is this:—Do these miracles, or do they not, redound to the honour of God? Is this miraculous process of healing consistent with our highest conceptions of the goodness of God?

Go back and look at the picture given us in the Gospels. What do you see? A man, apparently like ourselves, healing every sickness and every disease among the people; not only so, but giving power to his disciples to do likewise and even to raise the dead. Well, this man must be more than man; he must have powers unspeakably greater than our powers; for he not only heals every sickness and cures every pain, but knows how to do it without having learnt the art in any way; he knows it intuitively and does it all by his word or by his touch. So wonderful is this unlikeness to all other men, that a poor woman, crouching behind him in the crowd, finds herself instantly cured of a life-long malady by just touching the hem of his garment; the woman is healed before Jesus can discover who it was that touched him. Not a trace of medicine or healing appliances, such as ointment or friction is ever heard of, except in one solitary case of a cure of blindness, when Jesus made ointment of clay which he had moistened with his mouth. It is all magic, done without the smallest effort or pain to himself, without any outward agency beyond the word of his lips or the touch of his hand.

How vast a contrast is here presented to the laborious and hazardous lives led by our own healers of disease. Christ never caught any infection from the fevers and leprosy which he cured. But our doctors and nurses frequently suffer severely from contagion. They carry their lives in their hands, and with a magnificent scorn of their own safety will run many a risk of sickness and death that they may save the dying. Never can we forget such heroes as that noble Samuel Rabbeth, who deliberately sucked the diphtheritic poison from a child's throat, as the last and only chance of cure, and died from the disease himself in consequence. Here was a glorious martyrdom indeed; and like the life of Father Damien and Sister Rosa among the lepers, it throws the miracles of Christ into the shade. Then remember that this man, so supremely powerful in his magic, not only performs all these feats himself, but is reported, without a shade of surprise or wonder on the writer's part, as having given precisely the same powers to his chosen disciples, telling them to heal the sick, to cleanse lepers, to cast out devils, and to raise the dead. Of course people will say, such a man must have been a God. Only one in a thousand persons would hesitate to acknowledge this, if all that story is true. But now we must add this to our picture. We must look at the wonder-working Christ as a God: and it is here that the moral test comes in and shakes our faith in the picture as a Revelation of the Divine dealings.

We must first ask, what was the probable object of these miracles of healing? I say "probable" because there may have been more than one object. We are told in Matthew that these miracles were performed to fulfil a prophecy, "Himself took our infirmities and bare our sicknesses"; but we have already seen that this prophecy could only apply to ordinary human healers and not to Christ at all, who never caught any disease, who never became blind, or deaf, or lame in the place of those whom he cured.

The purpose may have been simply to do good and to confer benefit upon sufferers. Or, it may have been merely for the sake of proving the worker to be a superhuman and divine being. Let us examine this alternative first.

Among men it has always been accounted a glory and honour to be able to do something which no one else can do: and in the earlier and more childish stages of our race, any deed or exploit performed which was unusual and wonderful, and the agency of which was not manifest, entitled the performer to the credit of being endowed with super-human knowledge and power. The miracle-worker was master for the time being. Even now we have not quite outgrown this feeling of awe, reverence, or admiration for the magicians and conjurors. We love to be mystified, to see feats of skill and sleight-of-hand, which we could not possibly execute ourselves; and to this day hundreds of even educated people throng to the séances and to the mediums who can work some kind of magic or miracle to amaze and electrify them. There is a doctor who not long ago had quite a triumphal march through our provinces by nothing else than working miracles of healing. Whether his cures were genuine or not made no difference, he found thousands to believe in him and to honour him for his super-human powers and knowledge. Thinking to honour God in the same kind of way, men have taken the miraculous powers attributed to Christ to be proofs of his Godhead. They really think a miracle to be a greater honour and glory to God than the stupendous and silent forces of the universe which are exercised in accordance with inflexible law and invariable order. But this very thought of a miracle-working Deity really dishonours God and represents Him as a mere juggler, trying to amuse or astonish children. This thought belittles God to a shameful depth and drives away the higher thought of His real magnificence and glory which the constant order and law of the universe ought ever to keep in remembrance. Miracles, therefore, on the part of God, are open to this objection on moral grounds. They give a very low conception of God's thoughts and God's ways, they put Him on a level with the conjuror and the juggler, who, with all their skill and deftness, are now relegated to a very humble position among the world's great men. The feats now performed by true knowledge, by applied Science, and by the use of agencies every one of which can be properly and naturally explained, redound infinitely more to the honour and glory of man than any recorded miracles. So we cannot any longer ascribe actions to God which place Him virtually below the level of what is recognised as highest among men. It does not necessarily follow that our highest thoughts of God are wholly true, but it does necessarily follow that all thoughts of Him *below our highest* are certainly false. If, then, the miracles of Christ actually took place, God had nothing to do with them as evidences of His presence and power, and He certainly was not honoured or glorified by their occurrence.

We turn now to the other object for which miracles of healing may have been performed. This object was to confer benefit on the sufferers. We lay it down as an axiom that, whatever God does, it must be to do good; and we will assume that every miracle of healing was designed to give instant and permanent relief to the sufferer. It is this which kindles our sympathy and quickens our active desire to imitate the goodwill of Christ whenever we read of his works of compassion and kindness. Do not forget that he was a God; we must assume that he was, because these miracles are urged in proof that he was God. Now, what do we see in the Gospels? We see a man-God, giving proof before the eyes of living men that, whenever he likes, he can come to live on the earth, and just as he walks about from place to place can heal every sickness and every disease that comes in his way; and all this without any effort or trouble, with a mere word spoken, or a finger touching, sometimes with only the sweep of his robe through the surging crowds. He could do all this for three years out of a divine life of thirty-three and in one little corner of the Roman Empire, confining his gracious benefits to a mere handful out of the suffering and diseased masses of mankind. And then he went away again into heaven and has never been seen here any more. He has never returned. The sick and suffering are left by him to our tender mercies, to our slender resources, sometimes to our lukewarm sympathy, anon to our toilsome and costly efforts —often baffled—to find out how to heal the sick at all. Our magnificent hospitals, and the grand and noble army of European, Indian, American and Colonial physicians, surgeons and nurses are only a poor and forlorn hope wherewith to face and fight the bodily sufferings of mankind at large. For thousands of years before and for eighteen centuries since the coming of Christ, we have been left to learn laboriously and to strive all but hopelessly to stem the tide of weakness and pain and disordered nerves, while he the Christ could just as easily tell us how to do it all, and teach us how to do it with our touch or word, as he taught his disciples—*if he chose*. We know he could do it, for he was here doing it 1,800 years ago; and we know he could come again, for he came once. And surely we cannot say in the pride of a perfected knowledge that we do not need his help in the healing of the sick. But he does not come to do this, he does not move a finger to meet this worst physical want of mankind, to relieve this crushing burden of pain and sorrow, to prolong the life of our dearest, and to raise our beloved dead. Had he not been here at all, in the majesty of his miraculous power over sickness and death, we should have no word of complaint. But he has unfortunately been here just to shew us what blessings he could confer if he chose, if his fancy bid him to do it, if his choice of some favourites fell on any corner of the world. If he can do this again, if he could have stayed here at least till the lesson was safely and thoroughly learnt, if his disciples had only been careful to hand down the secret of their healing power in place of some of their scorching, damning doctrines, *that* might have served instead, and been a compensation for the centuries of his absence from our woe; but no, he looks down from his seat at God's right hand, in blissful disregard of our costly and laborious efforts, in total indifference to our nursing by day and nursing by night, which costs many a life and shortens many more—all this counts for nothing with one who came to earth not only to heal all manner of diseases, but to teach and to empower his disciples to do the same.

Now I say that Christ, as a God, is seriously compromised by all this. His whole career as a worker of healing miracles furnishes ground for a moral objection against his goodwill to man. It is not morally right to be able to help us thus, and to show himself to be able, and yet to refuse to do it, persistently to withhold from us those benefits which he is able, and was only once willing, to confer during a very brief visit which he could at any time have repeated if he chose. If you see, as I do, the moral blemish here you will not any longer imagine that God, the real living, loving God, had anything to do with Christ's coming or with Christ's miracles of healing. That story, of course, violates the order of God's rule over us and His discipline of us by pain and sorrow—but that is *not* the point now. The point is that it would be unjust and unfair to all the rest of the world if God were to have been incarnate in Jesus Christ healing the sick and raising the dead, etc., for three years in one corner of the globe, and then to leave all the rest of us in total darkness, none the better medically or scientifically for his visit. If he came then, why is he not here now? We read in the Old Testament such words as these, "I am the Lord, I change not." "I have loved thee with an everlasting love." "The Lord, the most High, fainteth not, neither is weary,"—certainly not weary in well-doing. And if it had been really good for man, really kind and loving to play the part of a miracle-monger on earth, there never would have been any pause from that day to this in his merciful labour of love.

But it would not have been good for men, not kind or loving on God's part, to break the sequence of His own majestic plans. It is good for us to be afflicted. It is good for us to battle with pain, and sorrow, and sin, and to rise from the conflict into newness of life and glory, to have our compassion kindled, and our sympathy stirred, and our hearts ablaze with loving wish to help and comfort every one that mourns. It is good for us to grow into what God wishes and intends us to be, step by step, day by day, and not to be made perfect all at once by magic, or our difficulties blown out of our path by the conjuror's breath. God knew better what was good for us than Christ and the Apostles did when He left man to work his slow way upwards by legitimate use of all his faculties, by faithful performance of every little duty, and by heroic devotion to what is good and true and kind.

God is in no way compromised by the New Testament. His Divine revelation is written in the facts of life and in the powers of Reason, Conscience and Love, which are enough and more than enough to teach us all we need to know. And we are sure to go astray from Him and His truth, when we seek proofs of His love and care only in tales of magic and in the childish stories of the New Testament.

Lecture V.

BEFORE I go any further in my Lectures on Jesus Christ, it is necessary for me to clear up, once for all, the great misunderstanding which prevails in regard to my personal attitude towards him. I say again:—Of the real Jesus of Nazareth I know nothing at all. I have not a word to say against him, nor a word to speak in his praise. He is beyond our praise and blame. There is not a scrap of real and genuine history concerning him. If I attack or criticise anything, it is the fictitious Jesus Christ of the Four Gospels. These are the common property of us all. These we not only have the right to criticise, but it is our bounden duty, as witnesses for God and His truth and as preachers of righteousness, to say quite plainly and unreservedly what our consciences and hearts feel in regard to the words and deeds ascribed to Jesus Christ in the Gospels. I do hope, therefore, that this declaration of mine will disarm the wild and fierce prejudice against me which prevails in the minds of many Christians, who imagine that, in criticising the pictures in the Gospels, I am casting aspersions on the real Jesus of Nazareth. I do no such thing. I might still further claim to be listened to and refuted wherever I may be wrong. For surely no man living has done more to invite correction, or has been more thankful to accept it and to admit mistakes, than myself. I take for my text this morning a passage which I am repeatedly told that I have "misinterpreted." Let my accusers say what is their opinion after hearing or reading this discourse.

"*Think not that I am come to send peace on earth; I came not to send peace, but a sword.* Matt. x. 34-37. *For I am come to set a man at variance against his father, and the daughter against her mother, and the daughter-in-law against her mother-in-law. And a man's foes shall be they of his own household. He that loveth father or mother more than me is not worthy of me; and he that loveth son or daughter more than me is not worthy of me.*"

I have been taken to task sometimes by very dear friends for what they call a mistaken or one-sided or unfair interpretation of the sayings of Christ as reported in the Gospels. It is very important that you should know this and that we should consider together the justice of this charge. A dozen good reasons might be urged for this scrutiny, among which are the following :—First, any mistake of mine so serious as this would be an outrage done to the truth. Secondly, any one-sided view, if not actually unfair, tends to unfairness, and would most surely weaken the influence for good which may belong to other parts of my teaching. Thirdly, any distinct and well-proved case of unfairness, in this particular matter, is a wrong done to the dead, I may say, to the illustrious dead ; and in so far as it might inoculate other minds with a prejudice, it would be a wrong done to the living. These three considerations are enough, you may be sure, to have made me extremely anxious to be accurate, generous and just in my criticisms of the sayings of Jesus. But still beyond these there lies the grave injury to which I should expose our Cause by bringing upon myself needless obloquy ; as if the *odium theologicum* were not fierce enough already without giving it fresh and unpardonable provocation of this sort. This is a question then involving the competency of your minister on a fundamental qualification. To be wrong here is to be incapable, stupid and blundering. To repel anyone from our Cause by true and accurate thought and speech is a misfortune for which we cannot reproach ourselves, but to repel anyone by inaccuracy or untruth would be a disgrace. It is therefore my bounden duty to you, to the holy Cause to which we are devoted, and to the God of truth and righteousness whom we worship, either to clear myself completely from this charge, or, if that be impossible, henceforth to abandon a course of criticism which has been proved to be erroneous, partial and unfair, and therefore in the highest degree pernicious to the good work we have in hand. As a specimen of the accusation against me

I will read some words from a friend who, on all other points, heartily approves of my teaching :—

"As to your interpretation of the sayings of Christ, many of these sayings appear to you dreadful. You are willing to get rid of them by throwing them aside altogether as pure inventions. You say to us, if you wish to retain your high view of the character of Christ you must discard these. But we refuse to discard them, because we have felt their truth in our own lives : and if they were not said by Jesus, they were said by some one who felt their truth and power. And if they were said by Jesus they are not damaging to his credit, but exactly the reverse. We will not admit your method of interpretation as the right one.

. . . . .

"I, for instance, can perfectly agree with you in all your religious ideas, and yet refuse to discard these sayings, or to accept your interpretation of them.

. . . . .

"My opinion is still very strong that in pulling up the tares, of which there must be some among these sayings, you are pulling up very much wheat. I think that on this point your judgment has been warped by the fear of not being perfectly honest, and that in consequence you have taken an exaggerated and one-sided view of the matter."

Yes, before all things I wish to be perfectly *honest*, but the very next thing I desire is to be perfectly *accurate*. The text which I have read to you is actually quoted by my friend as one to which I have given an erroneous or unfair interpretation. It does not stand absolutely alone, but is a type of a class of sayings, which I own are very few but open to gravest animadversion. Now, I wish you to ask yourselves some questions about this passage, and, if any of you consider *my* answers to them inaccurate, I beg that you would kindly let me know the answers which you would have given instead.

1. Is not this passage found in a book widely believed to be the inspired word of God?

It is.

2. Are not the words attributed to one whom orthodox Christians have universally believed to be God Incarnate, and who is believed by all other Christians to have been a perfect man, if not more?

They are.

3. Do not these facts of belief invest the words recorded with a far greater importance than they would otherwise possess, so that it is much more necessary to discern their real meaning?

This is so.

4. Is it not a canon of interpretation of all utterances that that meaning which is most obvious, which does the least violence to the language, and which best maintains coherency of thought throughout the whole passage, is most likely to be the truest and most exact meaning, that is—to be the real meaning of the author or speaker of the words?

It is.

5. Should any distinction be drawn between language highly figurative and that which is prosaic, so as to modify our method of interpretation?

Assuredly so.

6. Is the passage before us highly figurative or is it prosaic?

It is not figurative but prosaic. It is true there is a metaphor used once only, and that is the word "sword," which is manifestly a synonym for "strife," "contention," "war," in antithesis to the word "peace." In all else the passage is entirely prosaic.

7. Are we not bound to assume, therefore, that the speaker meant what he said and did not mean something else which he did not say?

We are so bound, and we are also bound not to allow either prejudices or predilections to give a false colouring to the sense which the words convey.

8. In looking at the form of the utterance, can it be accurately described as merely a foreboding of some sad consequences of a given event, or as the announcement of a definite purpose which the speaker had come to carry out?

In form it is *not* a foreboding, but the express declaration of a deliberate purpose. The Greek language here used is admitted by all scholars to be the strongest form of words to express a definite purpose and is *not* a mere prediction of what would happen. In one verse only there is a grammatical prediction: "A man's foes *shall be* they of his own house." But when we come to look at the original version in the Greek text we find that the verb which alone gives a predictive character to the English is significantly absent. It was necessary to supply a substantive verb between the two nouns, and I find no fault with our translators for inserting a verb in the future tense, and thus distinctly turning it into a prediction of some consequence. But this one predictive sentence cannot be permitted to nullify all the rest of the passage and to blind our eyes to the plain literal sense of the declared purpose for which the speaker had come. And I repeat that any Greek scholar will tell you that the passage begins with the most emphatic words to express a purpose and cannot be twisted into a prediction.

9. Is it not a test, a good test, of the plainness of the meaning of any passage when it is impossible, or at least extremely difficult, to express that meaning as distinctly in other words ?

Surely so.

10. Then applying this test to the passage before us, can you find other words which will convey the sense of it as distinctly and as simply as it is expressed already ?

I think it is absolutely impossible. It is a masterpiece of language in the grandeur of its brevity, simplicity, definiteness and plainness.

11. Is the plain sense of the words pleasing to us or displeasing ?

It is deeply displeasing. For any one to say that he had come on purpose to bring war upon earth instead of peace ; that he had come to breed strife and opposition in the very homes of mankind, and to set parents and children in deadly discord, jars upon our moral sense and we turn with revulsion from him who utters it. It is a depth of evil which, if possible, is still incredible.

12. If the meaning of the words is so dreadful to us, what are our alternatives ?

We may believe that Jesus spoke them.

We may believe that Jesus did not speak them.

We may conjecture that he said something like them in sound but very unlike them in sense.

We may draw upon our own imagination till we have re-written the whole passage in new words of our own.

13. Which of these alternatives seems the most reasonable?

In my opinion, that Jesus did not speak them; for since it is difficult to believe any one so desperately evil as to have cherished such a purpose, it is infinitely more difficult to believe such a purpose to have been declared by a good man.

14. How should the words run to make their sense good and pleasing to us?

"Think not that I am come to send war upon earth: I came not to send war, but peace. I am come to reconcile a man with his father and a daughter with her mother, even the daughter-in-law with her mother-in-law. A man's own household shall be his best friends. He that loveth me more than his father and mother is not worthy of them; and he that loveth me more than son or daughter is not worthy of them, and would certainly be displeasing to God."

These are words worthy of the highest of all religious teachers, and would have done honour to him whom they call the Saviour of the world, the Prince of Peace.

15. Is there not another alteration to be made without so completely contradicting the original words?

Yes! The speaker may have said, "Woe is me, for while I have come into the world to bring peace and not a sword, yet mankind will fight fiercely, when I am gone, over my words and deeds. The canker of strife will enter into their very homes, poisoning all their happiness and banishing peace and love. My heart breaks to foresee this dreadful woe, and would to God I had never lived or breathed rather than I should have come to be a bone of contention and the foul spring of war!"

Now a really good man would have said and felt this, and would also have done his supreme best to preach the paramount duty of brotherly love, and especially of love and peace at home, and not to have breathed a syllable of such claims of loyalty to himself as he might have known would surely rend them asunder with bitterness, strife, and hatred. Alas! let us put what words we will in place of this atrocious utterance, we cannot make them square with it; the effort to get a good "interpretation" out of it is hopeless. The passage does not contain a syllable of regret or sorrow at the evil foretold.

Suppose now that the text ran thus: "My coming will bring war upon the earth. It will set a man against his father and the daughter against her mother, etc.," and suppose also that though these were the actual words in Matthew, I were to say they were not a mere prediction but a declaration of purpose and that they really meant this : " I came not to bring peace but a sword, I am come to set a man at variance against his father and the daughter against her mother." What would you say of me ? You would say I had wilfully twisted and altered the meaning of the original words. Exactly. And in like manner I say of you, if you take the original text which *is* a declaration of purpose and alter it till it becomes merely a prediction, you are wilfully twisting and altering the meaning of the original words. You are explaining them away and doing the very thing for which you wrongfully blame me. That somebody connected with Christianity did so speak as to send not peace but a sword and most lamentably succeeded in his malicious aim is beyond all doubt. Here are his very words before us in the New Testament. The author of this passage has done more than anyone to create the very disasters of family strife which it is the chief aim of true religion to heal and to avert. All we can say is that we hope earnestly that Jesus was in no wise responsible for the mischief.

Yet we cannot conceal from ourselves that many words either spoken by Jesus or attributed to him were calculated to stir up this deadly strife and to plunge families into fierce contention. The very passage we are considering is ushered in by the following words : " Whosoever shall confess me before men, him will I confess also before my Father which is in heaven. But whosoever shall deny me before men, him will I also deny before my Father which is in heaven," and then follows immediately, "Think not that I am come to send peace on the earth." On another occasion we find the disciples saying to Jesus, "Lo! we have left all and have followed thee. And Jesus answered and said, Verily I say unto you, There is no man that hath left house, or brethren, or sisters, or father, or mother, or wife, or children, or lands for my sake and the gospel's but he shall receive an hundred-fold now in this time houses and brethren, and sisters and mothers and children, and lands, with persecutions; and in the world to come eternal life."

<small>Matt. x. 34.</small>

<small>Mark x. 28-30.</small>

Now I am not disputing these monstrous claims but simply pointing out the natural effect of them. Whether the claims were true or not does not affect the argument. Christ is here represented as making the acceptance of himself, as Lord or Saviour or what not, a condition of being received by the Great God at the last. Salvation itself depends upon it, damnation is the penalty for rejecting him. This is the secret of all the strife, hatred, bigotry and persecution which have stained the history of the Christian Church. This it is which *has* set a man at variance against his father, and father against son, and mother against her daughter. In a roundabout way natural love has been bewitched into becoming an adversary between the nearest and dearest. The intense anxiety to save the souls of beloved relatives and friends has driven the adherents of Christ to persecute and torture their kindred in the hope of driving them into heaven and eternal safety. And often, too, a warped conscience has made relatives hard and cruel towards each other, quenching natural affection and filling their hearts with burning hatred. Woeful have been such strifes in the midst of a once happy home. Irreparable have been the ruptures owing solely to loyalty to Christ on the one hand, and disloyalty to him on the other. Whether he made these claims or not, I cannot tell, but that they were made on his behalf and put into his mouth and that they have wrought the foulest mischief and bred innumerable wrongs are facts which none can dare to dispute. The writers of the Gospels must have seen something of the dire discord enacted before their eyes ere they could have dreamed of tracing it to the wilful purpose of their master. If this was their Oriental mode of describing the indisputable and deplorable facts, all the worse for Christianity and for the reputation of Christ to lay the blame at his door and to assert that that was the very purpose of his coming.

I must with shame and sadness also point out that in these days and under our own eyes is perpetually being enacted the same dreadful drama of domestic strife, bitterness and hatred directly traceable to the claims attributed in the Gospels to Jesus Christ. I could spend days in recounting the various instances which have come under my own observation and experience. The fact is too well and widely known to need illustration. In every case the haters and strife-breeders are sustained and justified in their hatred and strife by the plainest language of the Gospels. In certain passages of the Gospels their Christ demands of them not only affection but supreme affection, not only supreme affection but exclusive affection. In another place we read, "If any man come to me, and hate not his father and mother and wife and children and brothers and sisters, he cannot be my disciple." Fond lovers are forbidden to let their heaven-born love for each other stand in the way of their love and loyalty for Christ. The mother must not love her helpless babe if it robs Christ of a single throb of devotion. The father must shut his door in the face of his own son, if that son will not confess Christ. The name is a Shibboleth only less socially imperative than the passport of wealth. You may deny or ignore the Father in heaven with impunity so long as you call yourself a Christian or an Agnostic, and call Jesus "Lord, Lord." Loyalty to him still divides, as ever, man from man, friend from friend, and tender-hearted kinsfolk from each other. It is ghastly to see how true those dreadful words are, though he himself may never have spoken them. Men have done and are doing, in the name of Christ, crimes which hardly any malefactor would do in his own. Let us turn from this sickening spectacle to see what the love of God demands from us instead, to admire the contrast which filial loyalty to our Father in heaven always inspires.

That God whom we love and worship can only

(margin note: Luke xiv. 26.)

be truly served by our love for each other. Nothing else will do instead. No sacrifices will avail to atone for our not loving them. No religious zeal will hide from His eyes the dark stain of our hatred and strife. And to all who really love one another, to husbands and wives, parents and children, fond lovers in the spring-time of life, the same all-Fatherly voice comes like celestial music saying, "You can never love each other too much. Never can you make Me, the Eternal and Loving Father, jealous by your affection for each other. So long as you know what Love is, and are not mistaking it for selfishness or idolatry, the more you love one another the more worthy you will be of being called My sons and daughters. If your love is of the right sort, the more you love each other, the better you will love ME, and the more you will deserve that I should love you. There is not a duty in the whole range of life which you owe to others which is not thereby due to ME. As you fulfil those duties to each other you are keeping My commandments and fulfilling My law. Be not angry with those who do not confess ME before men; be not angry with those who worship another god, a false god or some degrading idol. All alike are dear to ME and I am ready to forgive them, for they know not what they do. You have no excuse for not loving them, if I count them not as My enemies, but look upon them with compassion and love as My dear children."

You are a father, perhaps, and are set against

your son through some strong theological difference; you think he is going to the nethermost Hell for not confessing Christ. If you knew ever so little truly about the true God, the Father in Heaven, you would see first the impiety of this alienation, and, soon after, its absurdity. The true God, who has already amply redeemed the world by the human love which He has poured out so abundantly upon our hearts, thereby reveals a far deeper and higher and wider love than any Gospel or Church has proclaimed. For once to know that we cannot love each other too much, that we cannot please our Maker and Father more than by thus truly loving one another, is to enter a sphere of religious thought and feeling where all is henceforth peace and joy, and even in the darkest vicissitudes a fountain of undying hope. These human relationships are thereby transfigured, and our homes become the temples of the living God, our domestic lives the perpetual incense of a grateful worship. God does not ask us to love each other for His sake, for any imaginary impersonation or representation of Him. He bids us love each other for each other's sake alone; and the more we thus love, the more we shall learn of what He is and of what we are in His sight.

While the Christian Gospel teaches that we ought to grieve and vex our nearest and dearest rather than dishonour Christ, the Theist says, you cannot dishonour God by anything so much as grieving and vexing your nearest and dearest. Make any personal sacrifices; even, if necessary, bow yourself down in the House of Rimmon rather than break your mother's heart or bring strife into your homes. God knows I should be the last to counsel a base conformity with religious rites that are no longer believed in. But remember, such hypocrisy would never have been necessary to prevent strife and to gratify those we love, if the glaring falsehood had not been first proclaimed in Christendom that eternal safety, or acceptance with God, depended on our " confession of Christ." In any case we should honour most of all that man who will never let any theological difference betray him into an unloving act towards the members of his own family. Let us Theists at all events set the highest example in Christendom of that perfectly unreserved love and generosity towards our kindred which springs from and is fostered by the conviction of God's equal love for us all, and which will do more than all else to undo the frightful and innumerable mischiefs of eighteen centuries' belief in a ghastly falsehood.

It will be useful to read and to answer some questions put to me by a member of our Congregation, upon points in the foregoing Lecture :—

"Although a man's immediate relatives and friends have the best opportunities for recognising his merits, does not the closeness of his connection with them, and the fact that his faults and failures are best known in his private circle, often make them his severest critics and the quickest and bitterest in resenting his departure from themselves in matters of religion?"

I answer: Undoubtedly so; but the question

seems to me entirely irrelevant, for the statement of mine on which the question is based is that (according to the Gospel records) the family of Jesus were not "startled by the apparition of a being diviner far than they had ever yet beheld," as Dr. Martineau would have us believe. My reply to that sentence of Dr. Martineau is that the brothers of Jesus were not thus impressed, but on the contrary looked upon his eccentricities as marks of mental aberration. So far my argument is quite unaffected by the question before us. The question is altogether irrelevant. But if we consider the question by itself, we see that it is an admission that there were faults and failures in the character of Jesus which might account for, without excusing, the severity of the criticism and the bitterness of the resentment displayed by his family towards him. I would remind my questioner that it is a pure assumption to suppose that "departure from themselves in matters of religion" was the ground of their hostility towards their brother. Not only have we no evidence of that, but we have positive evidence that the ground of their hostility lay in his unbrotherly behaviour towards them, and his unfilial behaviour towards his mother. That is recorded where his mother and brethren came to a place in which he was preaching, desiring to speak with him; and instead of compliance he says: "Who is my mother, and who are my brethren? And stretching forth his hand to his disciples, he said: Behold my mother

<small>Matt. xii. 46. 50.</small>

and my brethren; for whosoever shall do the will of my Father in heaven, the same is my brother and sister and mother"—thus bestowing regard upon his followers above that which he owed to his own mother and family. A really noble and perfect nature would not have been soured by family criticism, or resentment of eccentricity. According to the very precepts of Jesus, he should have returned good for evil, blessing for cursing, and kind and loving prayers in return for persecution. One may excuse Jesus for the infirmities of human nature. But it is a very different thing to shut one's eyes to the infirmities and to pour forth extravagant eulogies upon the "startling divinity" of the man who yields to those infirmities.

Another question put to me is this:—

"Arguing from the Gospels as they stand, was Jesus wrong in accepting help which was often freely offered to him by friends and admirers who were grateful for his teaching?"

Certainly not. But the question does not cover the whole ground. There might be nothing wrong, although nothing very praiseworthy, in accepting such gifts of gratitude and friendship. I never uttered a word of blame on that ground. What the Gospels record is that Jesus demanded sustenance and alms on behalf of his disciples on the sole ground that he had sent them forth on a mission; the Gospels record not only that he demanded gifts of hospitality, but threatened woes, in the day of judgment, against all who refused to supply them. This, in my moral opinion, was wrong, and betrayed a degeneration of character arising out of an undue sense of self-importance which led to the infatuation that it was a crime to dispute his claims.

The third question I have to answer is:

"Were the Jews, judging from Old Testament writings, people likely to give forced contributions from fear of threatened unpleasant consequences should they refuse to do so?"

Whether it was likely or not, the threats were made and that publicly. Even if not one person had been forced by those threats into giving contributions, our inquiry into the superior divinity of Jesus would not be affected. The threats would have no meaning unless they were uttered in the belief that they would extort contributions. As to the probability of their having any effect, that would depend on the amount of fear which the person and words of Jesus had inspired. As the Gospels are so full of devils and Hell-fire, we may conclude that the atmosphere of Judæa and Galilee at that time was even overcharged with superstitious fears.

The fourth and last question I have to answer is this:—

"Arguing from the Gospels as they stand, *had* the world seen in any man before him greater moral beauty than he displayed?"

This is begging the whole question of the exact moral position of Jesus, which we cannot even discover by a very careful examination of the Gospels, as yet only just begun in these lectures. The real Jesus *may have been* the very best man who ever lived, but the only Jesus with whom we are concerned is the Jesus Christ of the Four Gospels. Our scrutiny may reveal more blemishes than we expected, or less. But supposing we could not find a single blemish, we should be no nearer than before to knowing, as only God knows or can know, what was his exact moral worth. And until we know that, it would be impossible for us to compare him with others, and we could not make this comparison unless we also knew those others as God alone can know them. Biographies are worthless in so far as they are inevitably defective. They never can tell us everything a man did and said; much less everything he thought and wished for and dreaded. A biography, however long and detailed, is only like a colander which is full of holes and cannot retain the liquid poured into it. The character to be described by it is sifted and strained, and in the process many things disappear, both of bad and good, which are essential to accuracy and completeness. The residue is valuable when the process is applied to cabbages, etc., but of very little value when applied to men whose true and exact moral value we are seeking to discover. Most gladly would I undertake to prove that Egypt, Assyria, India, Greece and Rome had produced specimens of moral beauty superior to that of Jesus Christ; but such an undertaking is foreign to the purpose of these lectures and would also be liable to the fatal defect of being only guesswork. It is only God who can truly compare one man with another and say who is best and who is worst amongst us all. It is enough for my purpose if I can utterly disprove from the Gospels the extravagant eulogies in which Dr. Martineau has indulged. It is a dishonour to man and a dishonour to God to say of Jesus Christ that " Of anything more spiritually perfect than the meek yet majestic Jesus, no heart can ever dream."

Lecture VI.

AGAIN I ask you for your pity and patience in the continuance of this course of lectures on Jesus Christ. For your pity, because the task is so unpleasant that only the strongest sense of duty could drive me to it; and for your patience I ask because almost all I have to say is already well known to you. My duty this morning inevitably leads me to attack the opinions and words of one of the greatest minds of this century; one not only pre-eminent as a scholar, philosopher, and religious teacher, but as a man of gentle and loving spirit, from whom it is a positive pain to differ. In venturing upon a criticism of anything said by the Rev. Dr. James Martineau, I am aware that I am exposing myself to a charge of what might be deemed sacrilege; that, except under extraordinary pressure, no one would willingly commit so great a breach of taste as to enter the lists against such a literary and philosophical Titan. But not even the oldest and wisest are infallible, not any are so absolutely free from bias or prejudice, or so emancipated from the atmosphere of tradition in which they were born and bred, as not sometimes to err in their opinion, to be even faulty in sentiment, and to speak in open violence to obvious fact. In a little tract, entitled *Five Points of Christian Faith*, Dr. Martineau has again * given us, in his own choice language and with his wonted cogency of argument, a re-statement of some of the essential truths of Theism, for which we can hardly be too grateful. But in Parts 4 and 5 he has spoken of Jesus Christ in terms which not only cannot be verified, but are openly contradicted by the Gospel records. In plain language, if those Gospels give a true picture of Jesus Christ, and an accurate report of his words, then what Dr. Martineau says of Jesus Christ is not true; but if what he says is true, then the Gospels are mainly false. And again, if what Dr. Martineau says is true, he must have a solid basis for what he says, or else he has none. If no sufficient evidence be forthcoming, then we must infer that Dr. Martineau has received some special divine revelation concerning Jesus Christ which has been denied to us, and which contradicts the Gospels, or else he is drawing upon his own imagination, or repeating, without due regard to facts, the imaginings of other people. Any way, the sole justification for the present criticism is my firm conviction that what Dr. Martineau says of Jesus Christ is not true. I do not think any greater insult could be offered to an English congregation than to apologise to them for telling the truth. It is my plain duty to prove, from the only biographies

---

* See Preface to this Volume.

of Jesus Christ that are within reach, that Dr. Martineau's words are untrue. Let us first hear what he says :—

"While regarding the human conscience as the only inward revealer of God, we have faith in *Christ as the revealer* of His (*i.e.* God's) moral perfection. We conceive that Jesus of Nazareth lived and died, not to *persuade* the Father, not to *appease* the Father, not to make a sanguinary *purchase* from the Father, but simply to *show* us the Father (John xiv. 8, xvi. 25) ; to leave upon the human heart a new, deep, vivid impression of what God is in Himself, and of what He designs for His creature man : to become, in short, the accepted interpreter of heaven and life. And this he achieved, in the only way of which we can conceive as practicable, by a new disclosure in his own person of all that is holy and godlike in character—startling the human soul with the sudden apparition of a being diviner far than it had yet beheld, and lifting its faith at once into quite another and purer region. . . . . . . And so Christ, standing in solitary greatness, and invested with unapproachable sanctity, opens at once the eye of conscience to perceive and know the pure and holy God, the Father that dwelt in him and made him so full of truth and grace . . . . . . of anything more spiritually perfect than the meek yet majestic Jesus, no heart can ever dream. . . . . Jesus has given us a faith never held before, and still too much obscured, in the affectionateness of the Great Ruler, has made Him our own domestic God, whose ample home encircles all, leaving not the solitary, the sinner, or the sad, without a place in the mansions of His house. . . . . . This, however, is not all. His *direct teachings*, perfectly in harmony with his life, confirm and extend its lessons ; and we listen, with venerating faith, to his inimitable expositions of divine truth. . . Our Captain of Faith, having the highest sanctity, was enabled to speak with the most authoritative knowledge, and was inspired to be our unique guide, not perhaps in trivial questions of literary interpretation, or scientific fact, or historical expectation, but in all the deep and solemn relations on which our sanctification and immortal blessedness depend. And both to his person and to his teachings, do the touching drama of his life, the ignominy of his death, and the glory of his heavenly adoption, articulately call the attention of all ages, as with the Voice of God."

Now, all this is said with extreme literary elegance and force. It is true or untrue. It is only plain unvarnished fact, or a piece of extravagant colouring which, considering the issues at stake, is detrimental to the cause of honesty, of truthfulness, and of God. We cannot pretend to give the writer of these words any information as to the contents of the four Gospels; we can scarcely think it possible that he needs to be reminded of a single verse. He must know quite as well, and has probably thought over quite as much as ourselves, every moral blemish in the Gospels. So our perplexity is deep and dark indeed to know how such a man as Dr. Martineau could come to think and speak about Jesus of Nazareth in these terms, while the four Gospels stand open to refute him on nearly every page. No so-called "Higher Criticism" can account for such eulogy as this. For if every adverse word concerning Jesus were to be blotted out from the Gospels, even the residue, however excellent or even original it might be, would fall vastly short of the terms in which Dr. Martineau suffers himself to gambol. There is no accounting for the infatuation which besets even the greatest thinkers; and to seek for a cause in the present case would be as unprofitable as it is futile.

Quite another duty is set before us. Such words as we have to refute do mischief in proportion to their untruth; and in these days of gross idolatry of Christ, Dr. Martineau will be quoted, along with John Stuart Mill and Ernest Renan, as one of the greatest religious thinkers and teachers of the century. So long as any persons are left to set individual prestige above the rational convictions of their own minds, false sentiment will prevail, will be handed on from mouth to mouth, and be repeated until it is regarded as unassailable truth. Veneration—a feeling which every true man must value and cherish—ought not to be allowed to degenerate into a grovelling superstition. And yet this has been the fault of many ages, and had more to do with the corrupt elements of early Christianity and with its consequent spread, than any native love of truth and goodness.

For the sake of those who are not yet students of their New Testament, I must now point out those blemishes in the sayings and in the character of Jesus Christ which are indelibly written in the four Gospels. Some have accused me of having a personal animosity against Christ. I have none whatever. I only repudiate and condemn what his own followers have written, as they think, in his honour, but, as we now find, to his discredit. If Jesus Christ had not been set upon a pinnacle for worship, or been belauded with such extravagance by men like Dr. Martineau, there would have been little or no necessity for this display of the blemishes. It is to be hoped, and may well be believed, that the real Jesus was a better man than the Gospels represent, though one could not expect him to be enlightened above the age in which he lived.

In order to deal with this immense subject properly, we must classify our examination of the Gospel records.

First, we must look at the alleged facts of the life of Christ, what he did, how he was occupied, and how he behaved to his family, to his followers, and to the men and women around him.

Secondly, we must examine his words, especially his teachings concerning God and man and destiny, concerning devils and everlasting hell.

Thirdly, we must endeavour to ascertain his character by legitimate inferences from what he said and did.

Even this outline must occupy several lectures, if the scrutiny is to be done thoroughly. It is only necessary that we bear in mind at this moment and all along throughout the work, that this task is not a voluntary one, but has been imposed upon us by those who have claimed for Jesus a higher religious and moral perfection than the Gospels themselves justify. It is a task imposed upon us by the fact that Jesus is still worshipped by the majority of Christians as a God before all Gods; and by many who do not worship him as a God he is spoken of in terms of adulation which they would never dream of applying to any other human being in the world. Dr. Martineau has challenged us. We have no choice but to take up the gage which he has thrown down. He speaks of Jesus as

> "startling the human soul with the sudden apparition of a being diviner far than it had yet beheld"

and also says,

> "Of anything more spiritually perfect than the meek yet majestic Jesus, no heart can ever dream."

Dr. Martineau could hardly have said more if Jesus had been the Living God Himself; and if these his words are true, every man in the world is morally bound to imitate the words and deeds, and to strive to resemble the character of Jesus Christ in every particular. I can now only make a beginning of our scrutiny, and I at once proceed to examine what the Gospels tell us as facts and incidents in the life of Jesus.

The main bulk of the so-called history of Jesus only deals with his public life and ministry from the age of about thirty years. Of his previous history as a child and a man the Evangelists are silent, with only one solitary exception found in Luke. You all know it too well to need any repetition of it here. But I would fearlessly ask any father and mother whether they would like one of their children to inflict such torture upon them as Jesus did upon his father and mother. I would fearlessly ask any child of twelve years whether it would be right or wrong to follow the example set by Jesus in his childhood. We may make lame excuses for it. But we all know it was wrong, very wrong and very cruel. We know also that a really

Luke ii. 41-51.

loving child, if it had ever been so thoughtless, or so carried away by vain fancies, as to desert its parents for two or three days, would at least be bitterly sorry when its parents' agony was disclosed to it, and would have confessed its sin or error with deep emotion. But Jesus never uttered even a word of regret, but coolly asked of his parents, "How is it that ye sought me? Wist ye not that I must be about my Father's business?" (*i.e.*, God's business). He herein betrays the most profound ignorance of, and want of sympathy with, true fatherly and motherly love; also he betrays profound ignorance of God as a Father, who could never appoint as "business" to a child that which would wring its parents' heart with the greatest agony that can be endured, short of the moral ruin of their child. Yet alas! this story is read, and its false lesson applied to the minds of children by the million, who are taught to regard Jesus as a special and divine example for them to follow.

Of all the rest of his childhood, boyhood and manhood, up to thirty years of age, the Gospels are absolutely silent. His father was a carpenter, and it is presumed that he followed his father's craft. At best we can only surmise that he did, and that he thereby earned his own living. But from the day that he went forth to be baptised by John in the Jordan, and began his career as a teacher and worker of miracles, we have no evidence that he did any work wherewith to earn his bread. But if he had to live at all, somebody must work for him and feed him. Yet we read that both he and his disciples went about the country simply living upon alms, one of them carrying a bag for the purpose. We are distinctly told that in calling his disciples by twos and threes or singly, his first demand was that they should give up their lawful means of earning their bread, that they should leave their boats and their nets, or their office as tax-collectors, or whatever it was, and forsaking all must follow him. "Whosoever he be of you that forsaketh not all that he hath, he cannot be my disciple." It does not strike me as a pre-eminently divine form of perfection to adopt such a manner of life; and, as we read in the Gospels, it had a bad effect on Jesus himself and on his disciples, whenever people refused to entertain them as guests or to acknowledge their preposterous claims. Jesus told them that if any would not receive them, they were to shake off the very dust from their feet, as a testimony against them, adding "Verily I say unto you, It shall be more tolerable for the land of Sodom and Gomorrah in the day of judgment, than for that city." Hearing of these threats, timid persons would naturally be reluctant to refuse alms and countenance to Jesus and his disciples, lest they should incur a terrible retribution. The Gospels represent Jesus as asserting a claim for himself and his chosen disciples to be fed and supported by charitable gifts, instead of their working for a livelihood. And I do not regard this feature of Christ—universally present in the

<small>Luke xiv. 33.</small>

<small>Matt. x. 15.</small>

Synoptic Gospels—to be worthy of any great praise. On the contrary, such a habit of life is detrimental to character, and all the history of monasteries and convents and mendicant friars, based on the example of Christ, proves it to be so. At all events, it is not "startlingly divine."

And Dr. Martineau's eulogy is not borne out by the facts as recorded in the Gospels. If Jesus manifested such superhuman and divine perfection as to startle Dr. Martineau's soul simply by reading about Jesus in the Gospels, how much more likely to be startled with the divine apparition must have been his own family, his friends and neighbours, the population amongst whom he taught and whose diseases he healed, and the many good and true-hearted Pharisees who lived around and watched him. But instead of this moral wonder and admiration, we read of much unbelief in his pretensions; his own brethren, who knew him best, said "he was beside himself," and gave no credit to his claims to be lord over them. We read of criticism and answers and complaints, made by men whom we have no ground for despising or distrusting. After some of his outrageous or incomprehensible addresses, such as are given in the Fourth Gospel, it is frankly stated that "many of his disciples went back, and walked no more with him." His divine perfection, so far from startling his countrymen, repelled them, was not good enough to be attractive, was so mingled with denunciations, or so hopelessly entangled with

[margin: Mark iii. 21.]
[margin: John vi. 66.]

mystic utterance, or so offensively contemptuous of them and their religion, that it turned them into foes, blinded their eyes even to the good points in his teaching, and set up a hostility which ended at last in his seizure and crucifixion. The Gospels say how frequently he was rejected, and they bear proof of it in the frequency and severity of the denunciations which he poured forth, apparently in a spirit of mortification and wounded pride, against those who rejected him. All this must be accepted in evidence that many people who were face to face with Jesus and in personal contact with him, and who were therefore more likely to know his character, were not attracted, still less " startled with the sudden apparition of a being diviner far than they had yet beheld," but were actually repelled by it; while some of his own relatives accounted charitably for his eccentricities by attributing them to mental derangement. These ideas are not my invention, but simply what the Gospels disclose to us.

May the God of truth and love help us in this odious task, to do it fairly and charitably! I will only add that I shall be very sincerely thankful if any hearer or reader of these lectures will correct a single error or falsehood which I may unwittingly commit.

Lecture VII.

In the last lecture, I brought forward Dr. Martineau's eulogy of Jesus Christ in order to test its truth and value by the testimony of the Gospels themselves. I said we should have to examine them first as to the life and deeds of Jesus, secondly, as to his words and teachings, and finally draw an inference as to his real character from the testimony thus disclosed. Of course, I am not bound to touch upon anything but the blemishes: for the main object of these Lectures is to disprove the claim that Jesus was spiritually and morally perfect as a teacher and as a man. Nevertheless, it must not be forgotten that I have quite as true and deep an admiration for all that is good in the life and deeds of Jesus as Dr. Martineau or the most orthodox Christian has. The really good and lovely traits in words and deeds are not in dispute. What alone is disputed is that there were no blemishes and that—

"Of anything more spiritually perfect than the meek yet majestic Jesus, no heart can ever dream."

This is the misstatement and misconception which it is my duty to dissect and refute out of the Gospel records.

The first public act of Jesus on record is his coming to John to be baptized. Of course there is no blemish here, but it is needful to point out that there was not the least novelty or superiority in the message of Jesus, " Repent ye, for the kingdom of heaven is at hand." There was nothing startlingly divine in the apparition of a teacher who simply repeated his preceptor's or predecessor's words. It is true that the " kingdom of heaven," or " kingdom of God," are very vague terms; that is to say, they are ambiguously used in the New Testament. On one occasion Jesus said " The kingdom of God is *within you*," [but even this phrase may be rendered, as the Revised Version puts in the margin, "The kingdom of God is in the midst of you," *i.e.*, present among you]. But this is the only place where such a sentiment can be found on his lips, while the idea of the kingdom generally uppermost and apparent in the Gospels is a temporal kingdom here on earth, one that would fulfil the hopes of the Jewish people and be the work of a Messiah sitting on the throne of David. The twelve apostles (including Judas) were to "sit on twelve thrones, judging the twelve tribes of Israel." All those who had followed Christ and forsaken their families, and lands, and houses, etc., for his sake, were to receive "now in this life" houses and brethren and sisters and mothers and children and lands, a hundredfold for what they had forsaken. The whole atmosphere surrounding this term " the kingdom of heaven " was of the earth, earthy.

<small>Matt. iv. 17.</small>
<small>Luke xvii. 21.</small>
<small>Matt. xix. 28.</small>
<small>Mark x. 30.</small>

With the solitary exception I have quoted, Jesus distinctly encouraged, if he did not create, the conviction in the apostles' minds that the new kingdom of heaven was to be mundane, visible here on earth. And this impression was confirmed and emphatically expressed in the Acts of the Apostles, and in most of their Epistles, for they expected the speedy return of Christ to this planet. And we have to consider this in connection with the fact recorded of him that he began his ministry with the proclamation, "Repent ye, for the kingdom of heaven is at hand." He expected it to be on earth. He spoke of himself as its future king. He foretold his own return to it in the lifetime of some of his followers.

<small>Matt. xvi. 28.</small>

Immediately after the baptism came the fast of forty days and forty nights and the temptation in the wilderness. I have only words of high commendation for the spirit in which that threefold temptation was overcome. But I do not see that it places Jesus altogether above and apart from many of his fellow-men. It is not an uncommon experience among those who look upon themselves as reformers, and who, in the purity and singleness of their first self-devotion, conscientiously and resolutely resist all unworthy inducements to seek their own advantage or glory, or to sacrifice their principles for the sake of success in their enterprise. The story of the temptation of Jesus, however, is couched in language which betrays a characteristic of Jesus from the very outset of his public career.

<small>Matt. iv. 1, 2.</small>

It was a conviction that he was somebody, or to be somebody, of very great importance. He was to be greater than Solomon, greater than Jonas, greater even than the Temple at Jerusalem. He seems from the first to have been possessed of this strong impression, if I may not call it this great infatuation, which comes to the surface on every page of his history and in almost every word of his lips. If my business here were to defend instead of to attack Dr. Martineau's position, I should suggest that the ineradicable egotism of these portraits of Christ prove that they are fictions and not true biographies; that since no sane man would cherish such conceit, still less give perpetual utterance to it, it was invented by very stupid admirers of his who wanted to make people believe that Jesus was superhuman and divine. But of course we are prohibited from building on such presumptions by having to accept, *pro tempore*, the Gospels as historical records. [Matt. xii. 40-42.] [Matt. xii. 6.]

After the temptation, perhaps the next incident in the life of Jesus is the reading in the Synagogue. He selected the 1st verse of Isaiah lxi. for a text, and after reading it he closed the book and sat down. He then began a discourse upon it of which the only words reported are these, "This day is this scripture fulfilled in your ears." Then we read that "all bare him witness and wondered at the gracious words which proceeded out of his mouth." And they said, "Is not this Joseph's son?" To which he gave answer, "Ye will surely say unto me [Luke, iv. 16-29.]

this proverb, Physician, heal thyself: whatsoever we have heard done in Capernaum do also here in thy country. Verily I say unto you, No prophet is accepted in his own country," and he recited the cases of Elijah visiting the widow of Sarepta and the cure of Naaman, the Syrian leper, by Elisha. To our amazement we read that "all they in the synagogue, when they heard these things, were filled with wrath, and rose up and thrust him out of the city, and led him to the brow of the hill that they might cast him down headlong." In all this there is no blemish on Jesus whatever; but the narrative flatly contradicts Dr. Martineau's statement that the apparition of Jesus as a divine being startled the human souls of those who had a few moments before, wondered at his "gracious words."

In the narratives of the calling of the disciples, which are of course hopelessly irreconcileable, we cannot but find fault with the demand made by Jesus upon them to renounce their responsibilities and forsake their business and their families and give up everything to follow him about as idle mendicants. In connection with this we must notice also the answer given by him to one who pleaded "Lord, suffer me first to go and bury my father;" but he said, "Let the dead bury their dead, but go thou and preach the kingdom of God." I confess that the divinity of this counsel does not startle me as far greater than any I have heard of before. I have always regarded Gautama Buddha's desertion of his wife and child as a need-

<small>Luke ix. 59, 60.</small>

less and cruel act—the worst blot upon an almost stainless life. It would be inconsistent, then, for me to admire Jesus Christ for demanding a similar desertion of wives and children as an absolute condition of discipleship. It may be ecclesiastical or monkish, but it is inhuman.

Having chosen twelve disciples, and also seventy more for purposes of propaganda, the instruction given to them is open to blame, and was at variance with his own precept, " Bless them that curse you, and pray for them who despitefully use you and persecute you." He said, " Into whatsoever city ye enter and they receive you not, go your ways out into the streets of the same and say, ' Even the very dust of your city which cleaveth on us, we do wipe off against you' : . . . . I say unto you, it shall be more tolerable in that day for Sodom than for that city. Woe unto thee, Chorazin ! woe unto thee, Bethsaida ! for if the mighty works had been done in Tyre and Sidon, which have been done in you, they had a great while ago repented, sitting in sackcloth and ashes. But it shall be more tolerable for Tyre and Sidon at the judgment than for you. And thou, Capernaum which art exalted to heaven shalt be thrust down to hell " ; and he winds up his address to the seventy : " He that heareth you, heareth me ; and he that despiseth you, despiseth me ; and he that despiseth me, despiseth him that sent me." Instead of "all that is holy and godlike," which Dr. Martineau affirms Jesus to have been, I see in these

_{Luke x. 10-15.}

_{Luke x. 16.}

denunciations an unholy and an ungodly temper, spiritual pride which is not attractive, and a spirit of resentment which is positively repellent. When has the good and modest Dr. Martineau ever so forgotten himself as to imitate such an example?

I am sorry to call attention also to the unseemly behaviour ascribed to the Christ of the Gospels. There are three instances of it which must be cited: his conduct to the woman of Syro-Phœnicia, his rudeness as a guest towards the Pharisee who gave him hospitality, and his rudeness and unkindness to Martha, upon whose generous services he was dependent as a guest. This story is so well known I need not repeat it. But perhaps the other two cases are forgotten or have not been duly noticed. The poor woman of Syro-Phœnicia cried unto him, saying, "Have mercy on me, O Lord, thou son of David: my daughter is grievously vexed with a devil." But he answered her not a word. And his disciples came and besought him, saying, "Send her away for she crieth after us." But he answered, "I am not sent but unto the lost sheep of the house of Israel." Then came she and worshipped him saying, "Lord, help me." But he answered and said "Let the children first be filled, for it is not meet to take the children's bread and cast it to dogs." Meekly she still pleads for her poor child, "Truth, Lord, yet the dogs eat of the crumbs which fall from their master's table." Then he relents, as though he could not resist such a confession of his own immeasurable superiority. But no gift of mercy or healing could undo the cruel behaviour and speech that preceded it.

And a certain Pharisee besought him to dine with him, and he went in and sat down to meat: and when the Pharisee saw it, he marvelled that Jesus had not first washed before dinner: and the Lord said unto him, "Now do ye Pharisees make clean the outside of the cup and the platter, but your inward part is full of ravening and wickedness. Ye fools. Did not he that made that which is without make that which is within also? but rather give alms of such things as ye have and behold all things are clean unto you. Woe unto you, Pharisees," etc., etc., and then follow more denunciations. Imagine Dr. Martineau being invited to dinner, first omitting a ceremony which was thought to be binding both on sanitary and religious grounds, and then turning round upon his host, abusing him for his punctiliousness, and calling him a fool! This might startle us, indeed, but not on account of its special and unique divinity. Eulogies like those of Dr. Martineau are of no great value unless followed up by imitation, which is the sincerest flattery. And I imagine that no good man would like to imitate the behaviour of Christ on any one of these three occasions which I have named. *[Luke xi 37-52.]*

I heartily join in the late lamented Professor Huxley's criticism of the moral character of Christ's action in regard to the swine of Gadara. There is no law, human or divine, to warrant such a violation of the rights of property. "As ye would that men *[Matt. viii. 28-34.] [Luke viii. 26-37.]*

should do unto you, even so do unto them" was significantly broken in this case by the teacher who gave the precept.

I also see nothing but arrogance in the way in which Jesus provided himself with an ass on which to make his triumphal entry into Jerusalem. In-stead of sending word to the owner of the colt asking his kind permission to use it, Jesus bade his disciples take it and loose it from its tether first, and only give an explanation if it were demanded. This was ill-mannered, if not openly dishonest. One who acts in this way does not startle the human soul with a sense of his superior divinity.

<small>Matt xxi. 2-3.</small>

In this section of our enquiry, it is proper to quote the following narrative: "While he yet talked with the people, behold his mother and brethren stood without, desiring to speak with him. Then one said unto him, 'Behold thy mother and thy brethren stand without, desiring to speak with thee.' But he answered and said, 'Who is my mother? and who are my brethren?' And he stretched forth his hand to his disciples and said, 'Behold my mother and my brethren! For whosoever shall do the will of my Father which is in heaven, the same is my brother and sister and mother.'"

<small>Matt. xii. 46-50.</small>

This makes it more easy to believe that Jesus said on another occasion: "If any man come to me and hate not his father and mother and wife and children and brethren and sisters . . . . . . he cannot be my disciple."

<small>Luke xiv. 26.</small>

At the marriage in Cana of Galilee we read that when the mother of Jesus told him that the wine was exhausted, he turned round and said, "Woman, what have I to do with thee? mine hour is not yet come." In modern English the exact equivalent of this is, "Lady," or "Madam," "this is no business of yours. I shall act when I think proper." I wonder if Dr. Martineau ever treated his own mother in that way? John ii.

One of the most singular incidents recorded in the Gospels is the following:—"He took Peter and John and James and went up into a mountain to pray, and as he prayed, the fashion of his countenance was altered, and his raiment was white and glistering. And behold there talked with him two men, which were Moses and Elias, who appeared in glory, etc. But Peter and they that were with him were heavy with sleep: and when they were awake, they saw his glory and the two men that stood with him. And it came to pass, as they departed from him, Peter said unto Jesus, Master, it is good for us to be here: let us make three tabernacles, one for thee, one for Moses, and one for Elias: not knowing what he said. While he thus spake, there came a cloud and overshadowed them, and they feared as they entered into the cloud. And there came a voice out of the cloud, saying, This is my beloved son, hear him. And when the voice was past, Jesus was found alone." Dr. Martineau says, "Of anything more spiritually perfect than the meek yet majestic Jesus, no heart can ever dream." Luke ix. 28-36.

To me this story of the transfiguration of Jesus is a complete contradiction of Dr. Martineau. Perhaps hardly one of my hearers up to this moment ever gave serious thought to the spiritual aspect of this narrative. If the event occurred, it revealed not spirituality at all, but gross materialism. It is hard to imagine any deeper confusion between things spiritual and things material than this drama exhibits. It is on the poorest and lowest lines of necromancy; it represents—and here I cannot go a step further until I have expressed my deep pity and sympathy for Jesus in being so grossly misrepresented—it represents him, I say, as resorting to the commonest devices of jugglery to produce a startling effect on the minds of his three chief disciples. Let any man of true spiritual instincts ask himself what possible spiritual good could come out of a transformation scene like that. "The fashion of his countenance was changed and his raiment was white and glistering." How undignified, how far from the majesty of mere manliness was such a puerile sport with material things! It only serves to reveal the extremely low and undeveloped spirituality of the originators of the story; and how unconsciously they have bedaubed the innocent and simple-minded Jesus of Nazareth with their histrionic paint. Herein he is divested of all spiritual perception whatever. His power of spiritual apprehension and discrimination is here turned to total blindness; and he is set before us as completely ignorant of the distinction between the spiritual and the material. It is just possible that in our own day there are people left who could be impressed by such a scene as the transfiguration, and who could believe in Moses and Elias " appearing in glory," whatever that phrase may mean. But if they think that such séances as this in any way conduce to the spread of spiritual and moral truth, they are vastly mistaken, and they have not even begun to know what true spirituality means. I honestly say out of my human heart, that I deeply pity Jesus Christ as a man for having such a story concocted and told about him by friends who could not see the difference between honour and discredit. It is, however, ascribed to him in what is called " The New Testament of our Lord and Saviour Jesus Christ "—a book declared to be infallibly true because inspired by the Holy Ghost—and therefore I was bound to draw your attention to it. To my mind, it is impiety to mix up the Living God with artifices of this kind, and to attribute to Him any share in this terrestrial conjuring.

Lecture VIII.

ONCE more I must remind you that we are not criticising the real Jesus of Nazareth, but the Jesus Christ who is depicted in the Gospels; that is to say, we have before us a supposed record of the life and deeds of a man, when all the while that record is obviously untrue and mainly fictitious. That fact we cannot help. It is not *our* fault that people have mistaken this Christ of the Gospels for the real Jesus. Neither is it *their* fault, because the Church has taught them from the beginning that the Gospels were true, and were divinely inspired, and that the Christ of which they speak is the only real Jesus. To crown all, there is no other source but the New Testament from which we can learn that Jesus ever lived at all.

Before leaving the subject of what Jesus Christ did and how he behaved, I must mention the incident of his entering the Temple at Jerusalem and driving out the money-changers and those who sold doves for sacrifice, overturning their tables and rebuking them for profaning the Lord's house by making it a place of merchandise. His words were, "It is written, My house is the house of prayer, but ye have made it a den of thieves." Now, I confess that my sympathies go a long way with the spirit of this act and feeling of Jesus. It is in harmony with all religious feeling that the place in which God is publicly worshipped should be kept free from the traffic of commerce, and it seems like a desecration to intrude upon it the seats and tables of money-changers and the birds and animals which were necessary to such traffic. But when we look more closely into the narrative we see how false it is, and that it reflects very little if any credit upon Christ beyond a zeal which was grown into fanaticism. In the first place, this traffic in doves and sheep and oxen was not carried on in the Temple at all, but only in the outer court, called the Court of the Gentiles. Secondly, it was legitimate, being sanctioned by long usage and the consent of the priests. So that these money-changers had a prescriptive right to be where they were, and to carry on their trade. Thirdly, it was necessary to the proper fulfilment of the prescribed worship. For many people, coming from afar, could not bring with them sheep and oxen, or procure pigeons on their way. For convenience, it was necessary to have victims for sacrifice provided on the spot. Clearly, then, Christ had no right to interfere with this ancient and lawful custom, still less to begin to use violence without a word of warning or polite remonstrance. It does not shine

Luke xix. 16.

out as a spotless illustration of righteous zeal. It is tarnished with the great fault of want of due consideration for others and a disregard of their rights. It is a distinct and strong instance of doing unto others what one would *not* wish done to oneself. And when the astonished merchandisers asked him for some sign or token why he should treat them in this way, he answers them by an enigma which they could not understand, and which he did not vouchsafe to explain. "He answered and said, Destroy this temple, and in three days I will raise it up." Naturally enough the Jews replied, "Forty and six years was this temple in building, and wilt thou rear it up in three days?" The fourth Evangelist, thinking to do honour to Jesus, says "But he spake of the temple of his body." Even if true this was irrelevant. But it was worse —it was using language to mislead. This was no answer at all to the very natural and lawful enquiry, What sign do you give us to justify your behaviour? The fourth Evangelist, however, seems to revel in the skill with which he invents sayings to put into the mouth of Jesus which show him in the worst light. According to John, Jesus loved to mystify his hearers, and to substitute evasion for straightforward answer. The whole story is a contradiction of Dr. Martineau's eulogy of the "meek yet majestic Jesus." Neither meekness nor majesty are present here, but the most offensive egotism, a zeal absolutely untempered by sense of propriety or by regard for others, and an undignified exhibition of

[marginal references: John ii. 19. John ii. 20. John ii. 21.]

rough behaviour wholly incompatible with majestic serenity.

If I mention the cursing of the fig-tree among the blemishes of Jesus Christ, I will not do so without a caution. If any real benefit, if any good lesson could be derived from the withering up of a tree, I see no wrong at all in the act, any more than in felling it with an axe. We cannot be so foolish as to impute human sensibilities and regrets to the trees. And spiritual or moral good is always to be preferred to material welfare. But the fault of Jesus was in the temper displayed, like that of a petulant child when it is hurt or thwarted. Ignorant or unmindful of the fact that "the time of figs had not come," and that the poor tree could not be expected to bear fruit out of season, he uses harsh language towards it, and, in fact, curses it, as his disciples said, which in my opinion was a very bad example to set, and I expect Dr. Martineau to agree with me. Nor was the object quite beyond moral criticism. For, although faith is indispensable to the achievement of any endeavour and is the background of endurance and perseverance, the manner of teaching that truth and the entirely misleading application of it to the working of miracles, was more worthy of blame than praise, and calculated to puff up his followers with vanity and pride.

Dr. Martineau has unfortunately appealed "to the touching drama of his life, and the ignominy of his death" as evidences of the unique divinity of Jesus.

Mark xi. 12-14.

Mark xi. 13.

It becomes our duty, therefore, to examine some of the details of the trial of Jesus before Caiaphas and Pilate, and of the circumstances which led up to it. If possible, we must divest our minds completely of any foregone conclusion, and forget the various reasons for the condemnation and death of Jesus given by ancient and modern followers of his, fixing our attention exclusively on what is recorded in the Gospels. For we have heard it said that Jesus went to his death to propitiate and remove the Father's wrath against sinners, to offer the sacrifice of his blood in expiation of the sins of the world. It was said, during the first thousand years of the Christian epoch, that Jesus paid the ransom of his blood to the Devil, to cheat him out of his claim to the guilty and doomed race of mankind. Since the days of Anselm till now, we hear that the price of his blood was paid not to the Devil, but to God the Father, to prevent Him from sending the whole race of us to hell. Now-a-days, teachers like Dr. Martineau distinctly repudiate those ideas, but repudiate them in the teeth of the New Testament and of the Church's creeds and liturgies. From the Broad Churchmen and Unitarians we hear, instead, that Jesus died as a martyr or witness to the truth of his teachings; that he gave that proof, the best proof which any man can give, that he believed what he said. And, however wrong some of his opinions may have been, for that sacrifice to honesty of conviction he must be for ever admirable and worthy of honour among the sons of men. It is a grand distinction to be a martyr, though not a few of the world's best men and women, before and after the time of Christ, have been martyrs too. Some were martyrs for science, and many more martyrs for heresy.

But all these various theories of the death of Christ must be put aside and if possible forgotten, while we look steadfastly at the Gospels, and see what they tell us about it. Our enquiry will run in two channels. 1st—What led to the animosity on the part of the chief priests and rulers, which culminated in their determination to put Jesus to death? 2nd—On what definite charge was he prosecuted, and what was said by him in reply to that charge?

The Synoptic Gospels, as you know, give a picture of Jesus in his public ministry very different from that presented in the Fourth Gospel. In the Synoptics, his collision with the chief priests, rulers, and scribes is comparatively rare. Some of his remarks in the Sermon on the Mount in reference to the law of Moses, and especially to the Decalogue, were certainly calculated to arouse resentment on the part of the orthodox Jews. Speaking of some of the commandments of the Decalogue, he says, almost contemptuously, "Ye have heard that it hath been said by them of old time, Thou shalt not kill," etc., etc. Any Jew of that period would be likely to be affronted by such language in reference to the law which he believed had been written by God on two tables of stone on Mount Sinai. Still more

Matt. v. 21.

would they resent his going on to say immediately afterwards, "But I say unto you"—putting his own authority above that of the Hebrew scriptures. In that Sermon on the Mount he wounds the susceptibility and pride of the orthodox and strict Jews by openly condemning their habits of fasting, almsgiving, and praying in the streets and synagogues. On more than one occasion he treats the Sabbath with what they deemed to be scant reverence and even profanation. He openly rebuked the formalism and punctiliousness of the Pharisees, who were the most respectable and well behaved of the Jewish community; he attacked Scribes and Pharisees and Lawyers with fierce invectives, calling them "serpents," "a generation of vipers," "hypocrites," "whited sepulchres," and "fools." Of course, there may have been, and probably was, some ground for the charges he made against them; but we have no proof of it whatever beyond these untrustworthy documents called the Four Gospels. All we can say is that Jesus is to be duly honoured and admired for his endeavour to reform any abuses, to relax the oppressive severity of time-honoured customs and ceremonies, and to bring about a greater freedom of thought and action in the sphere of religion. But however much and rightly we may admire him for this, it is quite impossible for us to follow the example of his method and the manner of his speech. It was not only wrong in itself, but a polemical blunder, to assail with abuse those whom he was professing to enlighten and to lead into

[margin notes: Matt. v. 22. / Matt. vi. 16, 3, 5. / Matt. xii. 1-13. / Matt. xxiii. 33. / Matt. xxiii. 27.]

better and higher ways. "I came not to call the righteous, but sinners to repentance." Surely in his view the Pharisees whom he assailed were sinners, the worst kind of sinners. ^{Mark ii. 17.}

The offence given by Jesus to the upper classes in Judæa was further aggravated by his indiscriminate association with the outcast and the depraved. This so grossly violated the sentiment and taste of his contemporaries as to fill their cup of indignation to the brim. For my part I think that this true friendliness with so-called "sinners" was magnificent, was so bright and glorious as to stand even now whole heavens above our fastidiousness, our proud reserve and our prostration before the laws of caste. But it is to be reckoned with among the causes of the hostility which he excited on the part of the chief priests and rulers. We are expressly told that the parable of the Pharisee and the Publican was spoken against them. The parable of the Good Samaritan was obviously a hit at the priest and the Levite. We have, however, one glaring excuse for their hostility running throughout all the narratives. It was the assumption by Jesus Christ of superior authority, and the claims of absolute submission which he demanded from every one to whom he spoke. There was not a spark of humility or modesty in any of his harangues, while several of his parables conveyed the impression that God and himself were arrayed in war against all those who denied his pretensions. Again and again he claims to be the only mediator between God and men, and

^{Luke xviii. 9-14.}
^{Luke x. 30-37.}

^{Matt. xiii. 24-30; xxii. 2-14; xxv. 1-13; Luke xii. 35-40; xiv. 16-24; Matt. xxi. 33-44.}

says, "I am the way, the truth, and the life, and no man cometh unto the Father but by me." "No man knoweth the Father, save the Son, and he to whom the Son willeth to reveal Him." "Whosoever will deny me before men, him will I also deny before my Father which is in heaven." And this temper, whenever manifested, would be certain to alienate the hearts of the best kind of people. Throughout the Fourth Gospel all that is most unamiable and repugnant is intensified both in quantity and quality. Jesus is there represented (let us hope mis-represented) as the very opposite of meek and majestic. He is never meek, and often undignified. He simply wrangles with the Jews, evades some of their most searching questions, and denounces them as "children of the Devil," as a people wholly cut off from God's family and God's love, because they will not acknowledge his claims. As there is so much to say, I will not attempt to reproduce here the ugly caricature given us of Jesus in the Fourth Gospel, but refer you to my seven sermons upon it in Vol. X. of *The Sling and the Stone*, which I will send *gratis* to anyone asking for it.*

We have enough before us to account easily for the hostility which Jesus Christ brought upon himself by his behaviour and speech towards the Jewish rulers and upper classes of his day. That hostility ripened into the desire to kill him. We cannot, of course, determine with any accuracy what was the precise act of Jesus which led to his apprehension

---

* It will be found in nearly all the Public Libraries.

and death. From the Synoptics it would appear due to his triumphal entry into Jerusalem, which we are frankly told was an artificial fulfilment of a prophecy adopted and carried out by Jesus himself. This was followed by the scourging of the money-changers in the Temple, an incident which the author of the Fourth Gospel places quite early in the ministry of Jesus instead of in the week before his crucifixion. The speech about "Destroying the temple in three days" may have stirred up the animosity of the chief priests beyond control. But the Fourth Gospel tells us that it was the raising of Lazarus from the dead which brought matters to a crisis; for that Evangelist tells us that the chief priests and rulers said that "If we let him thus alone, all men will believe on him." How is it that no one seems to have penetrated the obvious falseness of the story? If Lazarus had been really raised from death, no chief priests or rulers of any kind would have been so stupid as to meddle with a man who could wield such stupendous powers. No, they did not believe—they could not believe—the story. Yet the Evangelist gives their real belief in it as the moving impulse to seek how they might destroy Jesus. What a hopeless tangle it all is! Nevertheless, in a few days we find Jesus seized and brought to his trial before Caiaphas, the High Priest. And when all the accounts have been read carefully, the final result in which they all agree is this: that Jesus was condemned to death only and entirely on the ground that he had made

Matt. xxi. 4, 5.

Matt. xxi. 12, 13.

John ii. 13-17.

John ii. 19.

John xi. 48.

Matt. xxvi 65.

<small>Mark xiv. 64.
Luke xxii. 70-71.
John x. 33.
John xix. 7.</small> himself equal with God. It was for this alone that, according to Jewish law, he could be condemned to death. The judge, the council and the bystanders were all struck with horror at the claim of Jesus, and yet were exulting in the fact that it gave them the only pretext on which they could condemn him. The charge against him of being a malefactor utterly broke down. His false accusers contradicted themselves and each other. His life had been pure and benevolent, no one could throw a stone at him for his works of healing, for his kindness and sympathy with even publicans, harlots, and sinners. But behind all this was the rumour of the claim which Jesus had made that he was not only "The Christ" (*i.e.*, the Messiah)—a claim which the Jewish rulers might scorn and might easily forgive —but that he was the equal of the living God, that he was *the* Son of God, in a sense in which no other man ever was or could be. And therefore he had been guilty of blasphemy, and according to the law in Deuteronomy he was deserving of death. No one stood by to plead for him "*Non compos mentis,*" and so the poor dear innocent creature became a victim to his own grand delusion, and without even a thought of blasphemy in his heart, he was condemned to death as a blasphemer. But, be it remembered, for no other reason in the world was he condemned or could he be lawfully condemned to death by the Jewish Court. All the minor charges broke down. But no sooner did Jesus testify on oath that he was equal with God and

that hereafter his persecutors and judges should see him sitting on God's right hand, than the high priest rent his clothes and all the people were horrified, and he said on behalf of them all, "He hath spoken blasphemy. What further need have we of witnesses?" _{Matt. xvi. 64.}

The late Rev. C. F. Chase, Rector of St. Andrew and St. Ann, Blackfriars, in 1876 published a little book, entitled *The Trial of Jesus Christ*, which I commend to the honest perusal of all persons who go on repeating reasons for the death of Christ at variance with the only records within our reach.

Yet a few more words must be spoken about the trial before Pilate, without whose authority not even the chief priests and rulers of the Jews could have crucified Jesus. At the outset, his accusers urged Pilate to put him to death because Jesus had claimed to be the Messiah and to set Himself up as "King of the Jews." Pilate, having seen Jesus for himself, saw through the absurdity of being politically afraid of such a man as Jesus, and for some time argued with his accusers to forego their resentment and to let Jesus off with a scourging. Finding they could not avail with Pilate in proving Jesus to be either a malefactor or an insurgent, they drew their last card and said, "We have a law and by our law he ought to die, because he made himself the Son of God." Pilate could not legally resist this argument, although he hesitated long, until he dreaded a tumult of the people, who cried out, "If thou let this man go, thou art not Cæsar's _{John xix. 7.} _{John xix. 12-15.}

friend. We have no King but Cæsar." This decided him to let them have their evil will with Jesus. He then took water, and washed his hands before the multitude, saying "I am innocent of the blood of this just person. See ye to it." To which they made answer, "His blood be on us and on our children."

<small>Matt. xxvii. 24-25.</small>

After reading the accounts given in the Gospels, it is idle to say that Jesus was put to death for any other reason in the world but that he claimed to be equal with God. He died, in fact, for a delusion. We cannot blame, we can only pity him for this. But our very pity and charity are proofs that we regard that claim as false. And we all know how such a claim would be met if it were to be repeated in our own time.

Lecture IX.

Our duty now is to meet the assertion that the teachings of Christ were divine and perfect, or in the words of Dr. Martineau :—

> "His *direct teachings*, perfectly in harmony with his life, confirm and extend its lessons; and we listen, with venerating faith, to his inimitable expositions of divine truth. . . . . . Our Captain of Faith, having the highest sanctity, was enabled to speak with the most authoritative knowledge, and was inspired to be our unique guide . . . . . in all the deep and solemn relations on which our sanctification and immortal blessedness depend."

Now, in order to meet and refute these extravagant assertions, it will be necessary to furnish rebutting evidence from the Gospels; and to quote passages from words ascribed to Jesus which are neither divine nor true. Yet, in order to make this evidence of still greater import, we must first present all the teachings of Jesus which are both good and true. This, not only in fairness to Jesus himself, but to show how the bad and false teachings undermine, where they do not openly contradict, the good and the true. It will also be evident that even the good and true sayings of Christ do not entitle him to the eulogies of Dr. Martineau.

My course will be first to quote all the passages,

or at least to mention the chapter and verse of every passage, in the Gospels in which Jesus teaches the Fatherhood of God. And by this term I mean that God is in such sense the Father of all mankind, that every man, woman and child that was ever born is alike dear to Him, is safe for evermore in His loving hands, and can by no possibility be lost or damned everlastingly. The term Father, rightly understood, carries at least *that*. And I am willing to give Jesus Christ the full credit for meaning as much as that, whenever he speaks of God as our Heavenly Father. When I have cited these passages, which will occupy all our time this morning, I will in another Lecture cite, on the other hand, the passages in which he contradicts or qualifies that meaning.

Of course the earliest and most distinct teaching by Jesus of the Fatherhood of God is to be found in what is called the Sermon on the Mount, as given in the 5th, 6th and 7th chapters of Matthew. It cannot be necessary to recite at length every passage in which God is named as the Father; seventeen times in these three chapters does the name Father occur. But Jesus must have a credit far higher than that of merely calling God by that name. We find on examining certain rare passages that he felt its deep meaning, and even indicated to his hearers once how that idea of God's Fatherhood had sprung up in men's minds. Not only so, but he applied the truth to our common daily lives, and showed how inevitable is the connection between true religion and virtue, between faith and works, between filial love to God and brotherly love to each other. Indeed, it is when we see this application of the idea to the daily life that we reach the highest point in the teaching of Jesus. Let me now quote some of his words:—"Blessed are they which do hunger and thirst after righteousness, for they shall be filled. . . . Blessed are the pure in heart, for they shall see God. . . . Blessed are the peacemakers for they shall be called the Children of God. . . . Let your light so shine before men, that they may see your good works, and glorify your Father which is in heaven. . . . Love your enemies, bless them that curse you, do good to them that hate you, and pray for them which despitefully use you and persecute you, that ye may be the children of your Father which is in Heaven; for He maketh His sun to rise on the evil and on the good, and sendeth rain on the just and on the unjust. Be ye therefore perfect, even as your Father in heaven is perfect." _(Matt. v. 6; Matt. v. 8; Matt. v. 9; Matt. v. 16; Matt. v. 44–48.)

I must point out that the conception of God's Fatherhood in verse 45 is somewhat marred by the argument used by Jesus. He seems to forget that the sun rises and the rain falls on birds and beasts as well as men, and even on trees and grass and corn and weeds. In this case the argument proves too much, unless all these creatures have souls begotten of the Father. Also he seems to forget that these physical tokens of God's bounty and impartiality are no signs of true fatherhood any more than a farmer is a father to his cattle because he feeds and tends them. It is a poor simile at best; but it does not prevent my expressing an unbounded admiration of the counsel given and the assurance that the following of it affords the strongest claim we could have that we are the children of God. If we can love our enemies and return good for evil, blessing for cursing, we then and there give proof of our divine birthright, overwhelming and sublime, a standard not always reached by Jesus himself. But the precept shows the high ideal which Jesus held of God as our Father, and may be counted in his favour to correct the bathos of his illustration.

Turning to the next chapter (vi.) we find more open and direct teaching concerning our relation to God. Jesus here tells us that it is a heathenish notion to think that God will hear us for our much speaking, for our importunity, in fact; that God, being our Father, knows quite well what is needful for us before we ask Him, and so He says to us:—
"After this manner therefore pray ye: Our Father which art in Heaven. Hallowed be thy Name. Thy Kingdom come. Thy will be done in earth, as it is in heaven. Give us this day our daily bread. And forgive us our debts, as we forgive our debtors. And lead us not into temptation, but deliver us from the evil one (*i.e.*, the Devil). For thine is the Kingdom, the power and the glory, for ever. Amen." It detracts nothing from the value of this prayer or from the credit of Jesus to say

<small>Matt. vi. 7, 8.</small>

<small>Matt. vi. 9-13.</small>

that this prayer was in use in the Jewish synagogues fifty years before Jesus was born. It is found not all through in the same order and form of words, but the first half of it is exactly as the Jews already had it. To my mind, the first two sentences, "Our Father which art in heaven. Hallowed be thy Name," is a creed in itself, a perfect compendium of Theistic faith, so it be properly understood in all that it involves. If accepted to-day in its integrity by the Christian world, it would inevitably destroy and extinguish the essential doctrines of the Christian creed. It has its work yet to do in the overthrow of error and superstition. I call especial attention to the fact that there is not in all this prayer or in all the Sermon on the Mount the faintest allusion to the idea of intercession and mediation. Jesus Christ here definitely teaches all men to pray direct to their Father and only to plead his Fatherly love as a reason why they may be heard. Jesus also sees with a true insight when he explains the prayer "Forgive us our debts as we forgive our debtors." He says "For if ye forgive men their trespasses, your heavenly Father will also forgive you: but if ye forgive not men their trespasses neither will your Father forgive your trespasses." This is true in fact as well as just in principle. While we ourselves are unforgiving and exacting and revengeful, we cannot enjoy true peace with God or a sense of forgiveness and reconciliation with our Father. In all these things Jesus speaks

Matt. vi. 14, 15.

as a true Theist, as an unsophisticated, pious Jew of his time. Where he stands out as exceptional and brilliant is in his moral precepts of love and forgiveness and rendering good for evil; in which I do not hesitate to say that he does surpass those of his predecessors of whom I have any knowledge, excepting only Gautama Buddha. Most of his theology in the Sermon on the Mount is excellent, but it is not new, nor is it to be compared with some of the utterances of Psalmists and Prophets for rapture of expression. But his morality, his humanitarianism, is superb, and it must be confessed with shame that the best part of his teaching on this point has been systematically neglected by very many who have professed belief in him as a God.

Let us now see how as a Theistic teacher he leads men to trust in their heavenly Father and to cast all their care upon Him. Here we shall see that his counsel is perfect, but his arguments are weak, if not unsound. "Therefore I say unto you, Take no thought for your life, what ye shall eat, or what ye shall drink: nor yet for your body what ye shall put on. Is not the life more than meat, and the body than raiment? Behold the fowls of the air: for they sow not, neither do they reap, nor gather into barns: yet your heavenly Father feedeth them. Are ye not much better than they? Which of you by taking thought can add one cubit unto his stature? And why take ye thought for raiment? Consider the lilies of the field how they

Matt. vi. 25-33.

grow; they toil not, neither do they spin; and yet I say unto you that even Solomon in all his glory was not arrayed like one of these. Wherefore, if God so clothe the grass of the field, which to-day is and to-morrow is cast into the oven, shall He not much more clothe you, O ye of little faith? Therefore take no thought saying, What shall we eat? or what shall we drink? or wherewithal shall we be clothed?.. for your heavenly Father knoweth that ye have need of all these things. But seek ye first the kingdom of God and His righteousness; and all these things shall be added unto you."

I utterly admire the spirit of perfect childlike confidence in the fatherly love of God, which these verses express. Spoken to the right people at the right time they should do only good. But when one has said this, one cannot truly admire the wisdom or the logic of the arguments of Jesus. They will not bear criticism. Men are neither birds nor lilies. Even the birds sometimes fall victims to their own native improvidence. They sow not, nor reap, nor gather into barns. If they did, they would not have such a terrible struggle to find their food, as is the case sometimes, nor would they die of starvation in the winter as so many do. But men are not birds: it is men's business to sow and reap, to gather into barns, and lay up for the needs of coming days and years. To tell them not to be over-anxious, but to do their daily work and trust in the love of God to deal with them as He will, is good advice, is the best advice; but it weakens such advice to use for its support arguments so fallacious, so transparently weak. Then here, too, we have the defect in the teaching which I pointed out at first—the Fatherhood of God is taken as a relation to the body and not to the soul, a mistake made by so very many. If God is Father only of my soul, I do not claim the rights of a child for my body. While I am God's *child*, and therefore invisible and immortal, my body is only God's *creature*, to live as long as He chooses, to be filled with good things or to be in want of them, just as He thinks best, and to be cast away at death as an unloved thing. I am not going to turn round upon Him and reproach Him because he is not Father to my dying body while he is Father to *me*, a never-dying soul. But Jesus does not seem conscious of this most important distinction—not here, at least: and it would be unfair in me to eulogize, as I heartily do, his advice to trust God with all our temporal wants, and for me to say not a word to point out the misleading fallacy of his arguments. "Do not fret. Take no thought. Do not worry yourself. For your heavenly Father knoweth what things ye have need of." That is enough. Any other argument will only spoil the effect of such admirable reasoning. A man is neither a bird of the air nor a lily of the field, but a reasonable responsible being, whose duty it is to take proper thought for the morrow and its needs: nevertheless, because he is so constituted by nature, let him rise into the greatest reasonableness of all, and put his hand out for the Father to lay hold of it and keep him from sin and fear.

Splendid is the counsel, "Seek ye first the kingdom of God and His righteousness," though it is spoiled by the improper and fallacious promise, "then all these things shall be added unto you." Just at the moment when the words of Christ are lifting us above our natural and excessive regard for temporal things, and setting our affections on things above, bidding us to make it our first and chief object to help to bring about the kingdom of God and His righteousness, no matter at how great a cost to ourselves, our thoughts are dragged down again to the hope of earthly things and to the craving for temporal good which only with great difficulty can be expelled. And I am sorry to own that all through this Sermon on the Mount, the beautiful teaching of Jesus is disfigured by continual allusions to rewards and punishments. Even the beatitudes are tainted with them. Threats of hell-fire and promises of reward in heaven are mixed up with almost every precept. The splendid exceptions are, "Blessed are the pure in heart, for they shall see God," "Blessed are they that do hunger and thirst after righteousness, for they shall be filled," and "Love your enemies, &c., that ye may be the children of your Father which is in heaven." _{Matt. vi. 33.}

I come now to a passage in the 7th chapter which shows that Jesus Christ was aware of the true basis of Theism. "What man is there of you, _{Matt. vii. 9-11.}

whom if his son ask bread, will he give him a stone? or, if he ask a fish, will he give him a serpent? If ye then, being evil, know how to give good gifts unto your children, how much more will your Father which is in heaven give good things to them that ask Him?" This is in principle precisely what we teach as the basis of Theism— that God must be at least as good as we; that if we, being evil, are nevertheless fatherly to our children, God, who is not evil but perfect, must be infinitely more fatherly to us. We infer that the God who taught us all our goodness and love must Himself be unspeakably good and loving. Yet once more, Jesus speaks as a true Theist in this Sermon of his when he says "Not every one that saith unto me Lord, Lord, shall enter into the kingdom of heaven, but he that doeth the will of my Father which is in heaven," by which he entirely excludes the idea that men will be saved by personal devotion or adoration towards himself. He was taking here his proper place, and repudiated the idea that it was of any value to men to call him Master or Lord. The only thing to be cared about and reckoned as a title to the kingdom of heaven was obedience to the Father's will.

Matt. vii. 21.

I have now given you honestly all that I could find in the Sermon on the Mount to support the claim that Jesus was a great teacher of the fatherhood of God. And truly if this were all he ever said or taught, that claim might fairly stand. Let us now search elsewhere in the Gospels for sayings of Jesus of a kindred character. Jesus quotes from the Old Testament, "Hear, O Israel, the Lord our God is one Lord, and thou shalt love the Lord thy God with all thy heart, and with all thy soul, and with all thy mind; and thou shalt love thy neighbour as thyself. On these two commandments hang all the law and the prophets." Matt. xxii. 37-40. "Love ye your enemies and do good, and lend, hoping for nothing again: and your reward shall be great, and ye shall be the children of the Highest: for He is kind to the unthankful and to the evil. Be ye therefore merciful even as your Father also is merciful." Luke vi. 35, 36. "Go ye and learn what that meaneth: I will have mercy and not sacrifice." Matt. ix. 13. "Are not two sparrows sold for a farthing? and not one of them shall fall to the ground without your Father. But the very hairs of your head are all numbered. Fear not, therefore, ye are of more value than many sparrows." Matt. x. 29-31. "Why callest thou me good? There is none good but one, and that is God; but if thou wilt enter into life, keep the commandments." Matt. xix. 17. "God is not the God of the dead but of the living, for all live unto him." Luke xx. 38. During the temptation Jesus says to the Devil, "Get thee hence, Satan, for it is written, Thou shalt worship the Lord thy God and Him only shalt thou serve." Matt. iv. 10. "The hour cometh and now is when the true worshippers shall worship the Father in spirit and in truth; for the Father seeketh such to worship Him. God is a spirit, and they that worship Him must worship Him in spirit and in John iv. 23, 24.

<small>Matt. xviii. 14.</small> truth." "Even so it is not the will of your Father which is in heaven that one of these little ones <small>Matt. xix. 25, 26.</small> should perish." "Who then can be saved? But Jesus beheld them and said, With man this is impossible, but with God all things are possible." Here we must add those words of prayer in the <small>Matt. xxvi. 42.</small> garden of Gethsemane: "O my Father, if this cup may not pass away from me except I drink it, Thy <small>Luke xxiii. 34.</small> will be done." Also on the cross: "Father, forgive <small>Luke xxiii. 46.</small> them, for they know not what they do." "Father, into Thy hands I commend my spirit."

Among the parables of Jesus are only a very few which can be placed on this side on behalf of the claim. They are too long to quote. But I refer to them as indeed well known to everyone. The <small>Matt. xx. 1-16.</small> parable of the Labourers. The parable of the <small>Luke xviii. 10-14.</small> Pharisee and the Publican. The parable of the <small>Luke xv. 3-7 and 8-10.</small> Lost Sheep and the Lost Piece of Money. And <small>Luke xv. 11-32.</small> last, but best of all, the parable of the Prodigal Son, which is a perfect picture of the fatherly love of God towards His sinful children. It is simply perfect, and is an antidote to the whole Christian creed and scheme of salvation.

I have read through the Gospels once more in order to search for any other passage in support of the claim that Jesus was a great teacher, if not the greatest teacher, of the doctrine of the Fatherhood of God, and I cannot find one. The selfsame record furnishes us also with very much more in quantity which is subversive of the teaching set before you to-day. Common fairness demands that you should look as carefully to the one as to the other. Indeed, if you admire and love the teaching of Jesus when it is Theistic, and because it is so, you must in your heart renounce and abhor that which contradicts or spoils it, otherwise your admiration for what is true is not genuine.

Lecture X.

In considering the blemishes which are to be found in Jesus Christ as recorded in the Gospels, we must observe that the blemishes in character and behaviour are not nearly so great or so numerous as the blemishes in his teachings concerning God and His purposes towards men. It is as an alleged teacher sent from God to enlighten and save mankind that he is open to the gravest animadversions. Dr. Martineau's contention, which we are now about to examine in the light of the Gospels, is as follows:—

> "Jesus Christ's *direct teachings*, perfectly in harmony with his life, confirm and extend its lessons; and we listen, with venerating faith, to his inimitable expositions of divine truth. . . . . . Our Captain of Faith, having the highest sanctity, was enabled to speak with the most authoritative knowledge, and was inspired to be our unique guide . . . . . . in all the deep and solemn relations on which our sanctification and immortal blessedness depend."

On reference to the Gospels for the verification of these assertions of Dr. Martineau's, we find the following plain and repeated teachings of Jesus concerning God, and man's relation to God, and man's destiny.

John viii. 44.   1. That God is not the Father of all men; but some men are the children of the Devil.

2. That God deliberately elected or chose some men to be "saved," while the rest would be "lost." ^{Mark xiii. 20. John vi. 44.}

3. That only few would be saved. "Many are called and few are chosen"; some would strive to be saved and "not be able." ^{Matt. xx. 16. Luke xiii. 24.}

4. That salvation and the final favour of God would depend on the acceptance of Christ's claims, while it is said of those who did not believe on him, that they shall not see life, but the wrath of God abideth on them.* ^{John vi. 47. John iii. 18. John iii. 36.}

5. That the punishment of God was vindictive, and not for the healing and saving of souls. ^{Mark ix. 43, 44.}

6. That that punishment would be everlasting. ^{Mark ix. 43-48.}

7. That therefore the teachings of Jesus were for the most part based on rewards and punishments, and appealed to the self-interest and to the fears of those who heard him. ^{Matt. vi. 1, 4, 6, 18. Matt. x. 28, 41, 42. Mark x. 28-30.}

8. That he, Jesus himself, had come into the world for judgment, so "that they which see not, might see, and those which see might be made blind," and that he rejoiced and gave thanks to God for hiding His truth from the wise and prudent and for revealing it unto babes. ^{John ix. 39. Matt. xi. 25.}

9. That God required a mediator between Him and His children, and that Jesus was that one mediator. "I am the way, the truth and the life. No man cometh unto the Father but by me." "No man knoweth the Father save the Son, and he to whom the Son willeth to reveal Him." ^{John xiv. 6. Matt. xi. 27.}

---

* These words are ascribed to John the Baptist.

<small>Matt. xxi. 22.
John xiv. 13, 14.
John xv. 16.</small>   10. That all things whatsoever we ask the Father, believing, he will give us. "Whatsoever ye ask the Father in my name, I will do it."

<small>Luke xiv. 26.
Matt. x. 34-37.</small>   11. That the true following of Jesus himself demanded the uprooting of family love and the disruption of family ties.

<small>John v. 22.
Matt. xxv. 31-46.</small>   12. That God had appointed Jesus Christ as the judge of all mankind, and that at the Day of Judgment he would separate for ever those who had been kind and good and loving from those who had not. This was one condition, only rarely laid down, but another condition often given and laid down by <small>Matt. x. 33.</small> him was that only those who believed on him were to have eternal life and the welcome of the Father, <small>Luke xii. 8, 9.</small> while those who did not believe on him, and who denied him on earth, would never see life, but be denied by the Father before men and angels, and remain under His abiding wrath.

<small>Matt. xvii. 18, 21.</small>   13. That the Devil and devils were actively engaged in the production of disease in the bodies of men. That they could possess or inhabit men, <small>Matt. viii. 31, 23.</small> and be transferred by his will to swine, or be otherwise cast out. It is impossible to eliminate this doctrine of devils and the doctrine of Hell from the Gospel records of the teaching of Christ.

<small>John v. 25, 28, 29.</small>   14. That he taught the resurrection of the body, and that at the Day of Judgment all men would arise with their bodies to give an account of what they had done and spoken.

    I have already, in Lecture IX, set before you all

the recorded sayings of Jesus which can fairly be accepted as involving the doctrine of the Fatherhood of God. They are not only few and for the most part concentrated in the Sermon on the Mount, but parallel passages in other parts of the Gospels are quite rare, and form no appreciable quantity when compared with the bulk of his teaching. I have asserted that the bulk of his teaching is subversive of the belief in the true Fatherhood of God over all men; and that the emphasis is laid on doctrines and ideas which considerably modify it or destroy it altogether. If this assertion can be verified by quotations from the words attributed to Jesus in the Gospels, then it is not true that he was "inspired to be our unique guide" in matters of religion. I am, of course, bound to go there for my proofs, seeing that there is no other record at all of what he said and did.

Let us recall first the interpretation of the Fatherhood of God (already adopted) which I have already credited Jesus with having sometimes taught, viz.: That every man, woman, and child of the human race is a child of God and is safe for evermore in His loving hands. Now, when we leave the Sermon on the Mount, there is scarcely a trace of that doctrine in all the rest of the Gospels. On examining the bulk of his teaching, I find that Jesus emphatically divides mankind into two classes, the saved and the lost, children of God and children of the Devil. And if ever he speaks of the whole world being saved, the conditions or the means of such salvation are inconsistent with a true fatherly love of God for each soul. I find the first indication of this division of mankind in the Sermon on the Mount itself. Jesus says " Whosoever shall say to his brother, Thou fool, shall be in danger of hell-fire." This shows that Jesus believed, as the Jews of his day did, in a hell-fire which was to be a final doom. In part of this very Sermon on the Mount he openly declares that only a few will be saved, and that many will be lost. " Enter ye in at the strait gate, for wide is the gate and broad is the way that leadeth to destruction, and many there be which go in thereat: because strait is the gate and narrow is the way which leadeth unto life, and few there be that find it." " Many will say to me in that day, Lord, Lord, have we not prophesied in thy name? and in thy name have cast out devils? and in thy name done many wonderful works? And then I will profess unto them, I never knew you; depart from me, ye that work iniquity." Do not fail to notice that these passages are from the Sermon on the Mount itself.

We pass now outside that charmed circle of higher teaching to the next chapter. " Many shall come from the east and west and shall sit down with Abraham and Isaac and Jacob in the kingdom of Heaven. But the children of the kingdom shall be cast into outer darkness: there shall be weeping and gnashing of teeth." When he sent forth his disciples to preach to the house of Israel he said, " Whosoever shall not receive you, nor hear your words, when ye depart out of that house or city, shake off the dust of your feet. Verily I say unto you, it shall be more tolerable for the land of Sodom and Gomorrah in the day of judgment than for that city." "He that endureth to the end shall be saved." "Fear not them which kill the body, but are not able to kill the soul; but rather fear him which is able to destroy both soul and body in hell." "Whosoever shall confess me before men, him will I confess also before my Father which is in heaven. But whosoever shall deny me before men, him will I also deny before my Father which is in Heaven." "Blessed is he whosoever shall not be offended in me." To Chorazin, Bethsaida, and Capernaum, he says, "It shall be more tolerable for Sodom in the day of judgment than for thee." "At that time Jesus answered and said, I thank Thee, O Father, Lord of heaven and earth, because thou hast hid these things from the wise and prudent, and hast revealed them unto babes." Whatever else may be thought of this passage, it certainly divides mankind into two classes, one which enjoys, and the other which does not enjoy the Fatherly love and teaching of God. But it is still further emphasized by the words which immediately follow, "Even so, Father, for so it seemed good in Thy sight. All things are delivered unto me of my Father: and no man knoweth the Son but the Father, neither knoweth any man the Father save the Son, and he to whomsoever the Son will reveal Him." "Whosoever speaketh against the Holy Ghost, it shall not be forgiven him, neither in this world nor in the world to come." We pass now to the next chapter, wherein Jesus gives a most excellent parable on the Wheat and the Tares, but utterly spoils and defaces it by his own interpretation, "He that sowed the good seed is the Son of man; the field is the world; the good seed are the children of the kingdom, but the tares are the children of the wicked one; the enemy that sowed them is the devil; the harvest is the end of the world, and the reapers are the angels. As therefore the tares are gathered and burned in the fire; so shall it be in the end of this world. The Son of man shall send forth his angels, and shall gather out of his kingdom all things that offend and them which do iniquity, and shall cast them into a furnace of fire; there shall be wailing and gnashing of teeth." Here we have the double assertion that wicked men are children of the Devil and not children of God; and that mankind will be divided at the last day into the saved and the damned. The same idea is expressed in the Parable of The Net — "The angels shall come forth and sever the wicked from among the just, and shall cast them into the furnace of fire; there shall be wailing and gnashing of teeth." The Parable of The Husbandmen, too long to quote, teaches the vengeance of God against those who reject Christ. The Parables of The Marriage Feast and The Wedding Garment, The Unfaithful Servant, The Ten Virgins, The Sheep and the Goats, all declare the final separation of mankind into the saved and the lost. A word is necessary on the last named parable. Here the judgment is made to turn exclusively upon the doing or not doing acts of brotherly kindness. In this aspect it is a beautiful parable; but it is marred by the same glaring defect of Christ's teaching, viz., the final separation of the saved from the lost. To some he will say:—"Come, ye blessed children of my Father, inherit the Kingdom prepared for you from the foundation of the world." And to others he will say: "Depart from me, ye cursed, into everlasting fire, prepared for the Devil and his Angels." In Luke, we have the Parable of The Rich Man and Lazarus, in which we read these insuperable words: "And beside all this, between us and you there is a great gulf fixed; so that they which would pass from hence to you cannot; neither can they pass to us, that would come from thence." This is one of the passages in which the irrevocable nature of the damnation of the lost is asserted without the use of the debateable word "everlasting." But over and above all these parables and sayings we have the direct assertion of Christ in answer to a direct question in the plainest possible words: "Then said one unto him, Lord, are there few that be saved? And he said unto them, Strive to enter in at the strait gate; for many, I say unto you, will seek to enter in and shall not be able." Where is the Fatherhood of God in such teaching as this? "There shall be weeping

<small>Matt. xxv. 31-46.</small>
<small>Matt. xxv. 34.</small>
<small>Matt. xxv. 41.</small>
<small>Luke xvi. 19-31.</small>
<small>Luke xiii. 23, 24.</small>
<small>Luke xiii. 28.</small>

and gnashing of teeth when ye shall see Abraham and Isaac and Jacob, and all the Prophets, in the kingdom of God, and ye yourselves thrust out." Matt. xx. 16. "The last shall be first and the first last; for many are called, but few chosen."

Moreover, when his disciples asked him why he spoke in parables to the common people and Mark iv. 11, 12. not unto themselves, Jesus answered, "Unto you it is given to know the mysteries of the kingdom of God, but unto them that are without all these things are done in parables; that seeing they may see and not perceive; and hearing they may hear and not understand; lest at any time they should be converted and their sins should be forgiven them." Matt. xxiii. 14. To the Pharisees he says: "Ye shall Matt. xxiii. 33. receive the greater damnation." "Ye Serpents, ye generation of Vipers, how can ye escape the damnation of Hell?" And to those who shall doubt concerning his own second coming in the clouds to Matt. xxiv. 43-51. judge the world, he says: "But and if that evil servant shall say in his heart, My Lord delayeth his coming; and shall begin to smite his fellow servants and to eat and drink with the drunken; the Lord of that servant shall come in a day when he looketh not for him, and in an hour that he is not aware of, and shall cut him asunder, and appoint him his portion with the hypocrites; there shall be weeping and gnashing of teeth." These passages are all taken from the first three Gospels, and are, in my opinion, sufficient to neutralise and spoil the other teaching of Jesus on the Fatherhood of God over all men.

If all these sayings of Christ are true, God would have to come to men to learn to be merciful, and men to go to God to learn to be partial, cruel and relentless. Nothing can be more clear and emphatic in these sayings of his than that he believed in an everlasting Hell, and that mankind would be finally divided into two classes, the saved and the lost.

These ideas of his are still further aggravated by his express declarations that this division was made in the eternal decrees of heaven, that some of mankind were "elected," "chosen" to be saved while the rest were foredoomed to perdition. This is not so prominent in the Synoptics as in the Fourth Gospel. But there are five passages even in the Synoptics where "the elect" are spoken of by name: "And except those days should be shortened, no flesh should be saved; but for the elect's sake those days shall be shortened." "The angels shall gather His elect from the four winds." "False Christs shall arise . . . . . to seduce, if it were possible, even the elect." Mark repeats the first two of these quotations, and we find one more independent passage in Luke, "Shall not God avenge His own elect?" which occurs in the Parable of The Importunate Widow and the Unjust Judge. [Matt. xxiv. 22.] [Matt. xxiv. 31.] [Mark xiii. 22.] [Mark xiii. 20, 27.] [Luke xviii. 7]

It is in the Fourth Gospel, however, that this doctrine of election is most offensively prominent. "The Son quickeneth whom he will." "All that the Father giveth me shall come to me," "And this is the Father's will that of all which He has given me I should lose nothing, but raise it up at the last [John v. 21.] [John vi. 37, 39.]

day." "No man can come to me except the Father _{John vi. 44.}
which hath sent me draw him." "There are some _{John vi. 64, 65.}
of you which believe not. Therefore said I unto
you, that no man can come unto me, except it were
given unto him of my Father." "Jesus said, Have _{John vi. 70.}
not I chosen you twelve, and one of you is a devil?"
"I go my way, and ye shall seek me, and shall die _{John viii. 21-24.}
in your sins: whither I go ye cannot come, Ye are
from beneath: I am from above: I said therefore
unto you, that ye shall die in your sins." He said
to some of his own countrymen, "Ye are of your _{John viii. 44.}
father, the Devil." "He that is of God heareth _{John viii. 47.}
God's words: ye therefore hear them not: because
ye are not of God." "For judgment have I come _{John ix.: 9.}
into this world, that they which see not might see,
and that they which see might be made blind."
"Verily, verily I say unto you, I am the door of _{John x. 7-9.}
the sheep. All that ever came before me are
thieves and robbers; but the sheep did not hear
them. I am the door: by me if any man enter in
he shall be saved." "I lay down my life for the _{John x. 15.}
sheep." "Ye believe not because ye are not of my _{John x. 26-29.}
sheep, as I said unto you. My sheep hear my voice,
and I know them and they follow me. And I give
unto them eternal life," etc. "My Father which
gave them me is greater than all." And then
comes in again that dreadful sentence about the
blinding of the eyes and hardening of the heart,
"that they should not see with their eyes, nor _{John xii. 40.}
understand with their hearts, and be converted, and
I should heal them." "I have chosen you out of _{John xv. 19.}

the world." In the prayer which Jesus offered to God he says, "I have manifested Thy name unto the men which Thou gavest me: Thine they were, and Thou gavest them me . . . I pray for *them*: I pray NOT for the *world*, but for them which Thou gavest me; for they are Thine." ^{John xvii. 6, 9.}

After these quotations I do not see how it is possible honestly and truthfully to say that Jesus was the greatest teacher of the Fatherhood of God, or that "he was inspired to be our unique guide" in matters of religion. In my opinion no founder of any religion that I know of ever said so much or so emphatically to contradict it. Therefore I do not listen, as Dr. Martineau listens, "with venerating faith, to these inimitable expositions of divine truth." I recoil from them as deeply untrue. This morning I have only brought forward evidence to show that Jesus teaches the division of mankind into two classes, children of God and children of the Devil, the elect and the non-elect, the many called and the few chosen, the saved and the lost. But he disparaged and spoiled the true Fatherhood of God in other ways, notably by thrusting himself forward as a mediator between men and God: and this assertion will have to be verified on another occasion by reference to the Gospels. If anyone is inclined to blame me for this course I will ask him two questions: Am I to blame for anything which is contained in the Gospels? Am I to be blamed for simply calling attention to what the Gospels contain?

Meanwhile let us not be carried away by a wholly controversial spirit. Hostility to those dreadful sayings of Christ is of no value to us at all unless it springs from true and fervent love to God our Father, and out of true love to our fellow-men. We need to be steeped in and saturated with a sense of the vast and unspeakable privilege of knowing and loving and trusting God before we may rightly venture to assail the prejudices, errors and superstitions of other people. Nay, we cannot do such work aright, we cannot do it with the earnestness and thoroughness which it requires, unless our love of Him is strong enough to drive us to it, to make it imperative, and to give us the courage to do it. But we get not such love of God out of mere books or head knowledge. It must come, if it come to us at all, out of our lives, out of the depths of experience, out of self-abasement and true sorrow for all our sin and frailty, out of a consciousness of His infinite Fatherly love and compassion, the sweet assurance of His forgiveness, and the promise of His grace in time to come. That love to God which is to be of any value to us as men and brethren must be first felt as a necessity of our daily life, the very breath of morn, the divine sunshine to banish gloom. We must know God not only by His bounty to us in our hours of gladness, but by His sustaining presence in our night of sorrow, and during our dark days of humiliation and shame. We must claim Him, not only one by one as *my* Father and *my* Friend, but as *our* Father and *our* Friend, the faithful loving Heart who watches and yearns after His wandering and wayward and wilful children, and will not rest till He has brought them all home. We must know and love Him as One who will not be at peace with us until we have paid our just debt of love and service to each other. We must know Him as a Father who will not be satisfied till we are right at heart, and trying to be righteous in all we think and say and do.

O Father, be to us a better teacher than the wisest and best of our fellow-men. Be more to us than any mistaken and misleading Christ. Be Thou the Light of the World, to dispel the gloom and fear from every soul, to make us contrite, to make us obedient, to kindle the fires of sacred love in these poor hearts of ours. There are those whom this day's words of mine will make angry and wretched. O my God! turn their hearts and open their eyes to see Thy truth, and give them heavenly strength and courage to cast away their idols to the moles and to the bats, and to come and take refuge in Thine Everlasting Arms.—AMEN.

Lecture XI.

In our examination, in the previous Lecture, of the Anti-Theistic sayings of Jesus Christ, we have already seen how the true Fatherhood of God over all men was completely destroyed by his repeated teaching that only few would be finally saved, and that the many would be finally condemned to everlasting fire; that some men were children of God, but that others were children of the Devil; that those who were saved were elected or predestined by God to be saved from the beginning of the world, and the rest were decreed by Him to perdition. I have asserted also that Jesus spoiled or destroyed the doctrine of the true Fatherhood of God by thrusting himself in as a mediator and intercessor between men and God, and this also I must prove by quotations from the words ascribed to him in the Gospels. Yet a preliminary duty has to be discharged. Some may be found to urge that although Jesus did declare himself to be a mediator, and a necessary mediator, between God and man, this does not detract from the Fatherhood of God. I say it does. It most wofully mars and spoils the whole idea of God's true Fatherhood. I speak as a human father, for myself, and I appeal to every father and mother in the world who have attained even the average standard of parental duty and love towards their children. If one of my children has done me a grievous wrong, or committed the most dreadful trespass against his brothers or sisters, so long as I have true fatherly love towards that guilty one, nothing would distress me more or make me more indignant than for any one to come and plead on his behalf for my forgiveness—as if any one in the world could love him better than I do. On the other hand, if I would not see him or speak to him, if I drove him away and refused to listen to his cry of repentance, and would only consent to be lenient towards him because of the kind intervention of some good brother or sister or friend, then I should know in my inmost heart that my fatherly love for that son was *dead*. I might try to excuse my want of love by dwelling on the enormity of his offence; I might even mistrust my powers of forgiveness if he came arrogantly into my presence. But with every pang of such emotions I should condemn myself through and through, and I could not honestly say I had any true fatherly love left in me towards that guilty child. Again, if any child of mine wanted any gift or indulgence, but would not venture to ask for it, sending to me instead his mother or some brother or sister to plead on his behalf; I well remember the shame and anger which such conduct aroused. I felt insulted to the very bone to think that any child of mine was afraid to come straight to me to ask me for anything in the world which I could give him. It was such a slur upon my fatherly love, such a disgrace to my fatherly heart, that I could not bear it with patience, and I could have wept to find myself so little trusted, so little understood. Thank God! such a dishonour never came to me but once or twice in all my life! But it is alas! not infrequent in homes where true fatherly and motherly love are lacking or feeble, and where parents have forfeited their children's confidence through injustice or cruelty. No true father can endure the idea of mediation. In one sense only can mediation be possible or right, consistently with true fatherly love. It is in a father sending some one to plead with a child who has by sin or estrangement lost all filial confidence in his parent. Then the father will send not only one but many mediators, any whom he can get to go and assure the child of his father's faithful love, and beseech him to return home. But this is only necessary between parents and children because we are human beings, and not able to be everywhere at once; and because our love and powers of entreaty and persuasion are all weak and limited and often inadequate to produce the reconciliation we desire. This necessity can never arise in the case of God and the alienation of His children. He needs no messengers to assure His children of His unwearied, faithful, fatherly love. It is only His Voice that can awaken the dead soul and quicken the undutiful son into repentance and return. Still, granting that God does use human words to bring

His lost children back to Himself, this kind of mediation is multifold. It is carried on by millions of such mediators, and can in no sense be confined exclusively to Christ. And no such mediator could be of any value at all, unless he told the simple truth of the loving heart of God, which was waiting and longing for the return of the sinful child. Christ's parable of the Prodigal Son is, in this view, perfect in fixing the whole attention and thought upon the Fatherly love which needs no mediator. Our quarrel with Christ is that he contradicted that parable by a vast number of sayings in which he taught the necessity of himself as the sole mediator between God and man, to reconcile our Father to us. This we must now verify by quotations :—"No man knoweth the Son, but the Father; neither knoweth any man the Father save the Son, and he to whomsoever the Son willeth to reveal him." "Come unto me" (not, come unto God your Father), "all ye that labour and are heavy laden, and I will give you rest." "If two of you shall agree on earth as touching anything that they shall ask, it shall be done for them of my Father which is in Heaven. For where two or three are gathered together in my name, there am I in the midst of them." "This is my blood of the New Testament, which is shed for many for the remission of sins." "Thus it is written and thus it behoved Christ to suffer, and to rise again the third day; and that repentance and remission of sins should be preached in his name among all nations." You will notice

[Matt. xi. 27, 28.]
[Matt. xviii. 19, 20.]
[Matt. xxvi. 28.]
[Luke xxiv. 46, 47.]

how very few passages there are in the Synoptic Gospels which definitely assert the mediation of Christ. It is only when we come to the Fourth Gospel that we find Jesus claiming in persistent language to stand between man and God. "As Moses lifted up the serpent in the wilderness, even so must the Son of Man be lifted up ; that whosoever believeth in *him* should not perish but have eternal life. God so loved the world that He gave His only-begotten Son, that whosoever believeth in him should not perish but have everlasting life. For God sent not His Son into the world to condemn the world; but that the world through him might be saved. He that believeth on him is not condemned ; but he that believeth not is condemned already, because he hath not believed in the name of the only-begotten Son of God." Observe that the term " only-begotten Son of God " involves the idea that God was only real Father to Jesus and to no one else. This, in itself, contradicts the universal Fatherhood of God. Moreover, the love of God for the world, so loudly boasted of, is immediately contradicted by the conditions laid down for salvation ; whereas the true fatherly love of God means unconditional salvation, and that, not from wholesome punishment, but from sin. It is also contradicted by salvation from punishment through Christ, as a mediator and a ransom. "As the Father raiseth up the dead and quickeneth them ; even so the Son quickeneth whom he will. For the Father judgeth no man, but hath committed all judgment

[margin: John iii. 14-18.]
[margin: John v. 21-23.]

unto the Son, that all men should honour the Son even as they honour the Father. He that honoureth not the Son honoureth not the Father which hath sent him." "Ye will not come unto me that ye might have life." "The bread of God is he which cometh down from heaven and giveth life to the world." "I am the bread of life; he that cometh to me shall never hunger; and he that believeth on me shall never thirst." "No man can come to me except the Father which hath sent me draw him." "Not that any man hath seen the Father, save he which is of God, he hath seen the Father. Verily I say unto you, He that believeth on me hath everlasting life." "I am that bread of life." "I am the living bread which came down from heaven: if any man eat of this bread he shall live for ever." "Verily, verily, I say unto you, Except ye eat the flesh of the Son of Man and drink his blood, ye have no life in you," etc., etc. [Compare this with the Lord's Prayer, and with those words of Jesus in St. Matthew, "If thou wilt enter into life, keep the commandments."] "No man can come unto me except it were given unto him of my Father." "If the Son shall make you free, ye shall be free indeed." "I am the door of the sheep. All that ever came before me are thieves and robbers, but the sheep did not hear them. I am the door; by me if any man enter in he shall be saved." "I am the good shepherd, the good shepherd giveth his life for the sheep." "I lay down my life for the sheep." "My sheep hear my voice, and they

<small>John v. 40.
John vi. 33.
John vi. 35.
John vi. 44.
John vi. 46-48.
John vi. 51.
John vi. 53-58.
Matt. xix. 17.
John vi. 65.
John viii. 36.
John x. 7-9.
John x. 11.
John x. 15.
John x. 27, 28.</small>

follow me; and I give unto them eternal life; and they shall never perish, neither shall any man pluck them out of my hand." Of course, this, if true, renders God the Father quite superfluous. Jesus said to the sister of Lazarus: "I am the resurrection and the life; he that believeth in me, though he were dead, yet shall he live; and whosoever believeth in me shall never die. Believest thou this?" [To which *we* reply—Certainly not]. "He that believeth on me believeth not on me, but on Him that sent me. And he that seeth me, seeth Him that sent me. I am come a light into the world, that whosoever believeth in me should not abide in darkness." "Ye call me Master and Lord; and ye say well, for so I am." "I am the way, the truth, and the life; no man cometh unto the Father but by me." "He that hath seen me hath seen the Father." "Whatsoever ye shall ask in my name, that will I do, that the Father may be glorified in the Son. If ye shall ask anything in my name, I will do it." "I will pray the Father for you, and he shall give you another Comforter." "I am the true vine and my Father is the husbandman." "I am the vine, ye are the branches." "He that hateth me hateth my Father also." "When the Comforter is come, whom I will send unto you from the Father, even the Spirit of truth, which proceedeth from the Father, he shall testify of me." "It is expedient for you that I go away; for if I go not away, the Comforter will not come unto you, but if I depart I will send Him unto you." Yet Jesus had said, in the Sermon on the Mount, that God would, of course, give His Holy Spirit to any one that asked Him for it. "Verily, verily, I say unto you, Whatsoever ye shall ask the Father in my name, He will give it you. Hitherto ye have asked nothing in my name: ask and ye shall receive, that your joy may be full." John xvi. 23, 24.

I surely need not quote any more passages to show the position in which Jesus Christ claimed to stand as Mediator between God and man, as, indeed, a very substitute for the Father. It is for the Christians now to reconcile this teaching with that other in the Lord's Prayer, and kindred Theistic sayings, of which I gave a complete list in the Ninth Lecture of this series. In the Fourth Gospel the aberration is full-blown, but, as I shall now prove, the germs of it are to be found even in the Synoptics.

It cannot be questioned, by either the Christians themselves or by their opponents, that from the beginning to the end of Jesus Christ's ministry he assumed an air of superiority over his fellow-men, and increasingly asserted that God the Father had delegated to him an authority which no sane man could claim for himself without bringing down upon him reprobation or pity. To prove this by quotations I am sure must be quite needless, and, if it were insisted on, I should have to recite nearly every word spoken by Jesus. But I will give one or two examples of it, just to make certain what I mean. "Many shall say to me in that day, Lord, Matt. vii. 22, 23.

Lord, have we not prophesied in thy name? and in thy name have cast out devils? and in thy name done many wonderful works? Then will I profess unto them, I never knew you: depart from me ye that work iniquity." "I say unto you that in this place is one greater than the temple." "For the Son of Man is Lord even of the Sabbath day." "Behold a greater than Jonas is here." "Behold a greater than Solomon is here." "Whom say ye that I am? And Simon Peter answered and said, Thou art the Christ, the son of the living God. And Jesus answered and said unto him, Blessed art thou, Simon Bar-jona, for flesh and blood hath not revealed it unto thee, but my Father which is in heaven. And I say unto thee, Thou art Peter, and upon this rock I will build my church, and the gates of hell shall not prevail against it. And I will give unto thee the keys of the kingdom of heaven, and whatsoever thou shalt bind on earth shall be bound in heaven, and whatsoever thou shalt loose on earth shall be loosed in heaven." "Whosoever shall confess me before men, him will I confess also before my Father which is in heaven; and whosoever will deny me before men, him will I also deny before my Father which is in heaven. Think not that I am come to send peace on earth: I came not to send peace, but a sword. For I am come to set a man at variance against his father and the daughter against her mother, etc. And a man's foes shall be they of his own household. He that loveth father or mother more than me is not

Matt. xii. 6-8.
Matt. xii. 41-42.
Matt. xvi. 15-19.
Matt. x. 32-37.

worthy of me; and he that loveth son or daughter more than me is not worthy of me." But all doubt on the vast assumptions of Jesus is at once closed when we turn to the passages in which Jesus declares that he will be the Judge of all men at the last day. "When the Son of Man shall come in his glory, and all the holy angels with him, then shall he sit upon the throne of his glory, and before him shall be gathered all nations, and he shall separate them one from another, as a shepherd divideth his sheep from the goats; and he shall set the sheep on his right hand and the goats on the left. Then shall the King say to them on his right hand, Come, ye blessed of my Father, inherit the kingdom prepared for you from the foundation of the world. Then shall he say also unto them on his left hand, Depart from me, ye cursed, into everlasting fire prepared for the Devil and his angels." There is a passage also in which Jesus makes this stupendous claim, and in the form of a prediction which has been absolutely falsified by subsequent facts and can never be fulfilled at all. "Immediately after the tribulation of those days shall the sun be darkened, and the moon shall not give her light, and the stars shall fall from heaven, and the powers of heaven shall be shaken; and then shall appear the sign of the Son of Man in heaven, and then shall all the tribes of the earth mourn; and they shall see the Son of Man coming in the clouds of heaven with power and great glory. So likewise ye" (the disciples to whom he was

Matt. xxv. 31-34, 41.

Matt. xxiv. 29-31.

speaking) " when ye shall see all these things, know that it is near, even at the doors. Verily I say unto you, This generation shall not pass till all these things be fulfilled." But these things were not fulfilled in that generation, therefore the prediction of it can never be fulfilled at all.

<small>Matt. xxvi. 63-65.</small> " And the high priest answered and said unto him, I adjure thee by the living God, that thou tell us whether thou be the Christ, the Son of God. Jesus saith unto him, Thou hast said" (meaning in our language, "Yes, I am"). "Nevertheless I say unto you, Hereafter shall ye see the Son of Man sitting on the right hand of power and coming in the clouds of heaven. Then the high priest rent his clothes, saying, He hath spoken blasphemy, what further need have we of witnesses? Behold now, ye have heard his blasphemy."

Now remember that the words of Jesus Christ which I have quoted are recorded by his own friends, and not made up by me, and the effect produced by them is also faithfully recorded. They sounded like blasphemy upon Jewish ears. I say that no sane person could speak thus without incurring either pity for a delusion, or reprobation for making a false claim. We cannot, therefore, subscribe to Dr. Martineau's effusive language about the Christ of the Gospels; we consider it impossible, because deeply untrue, to say that the words of Jesus were " inimitable expressions of divine truth," or that he was " inspired to be our unique guide in all the deep and solemn relations on which our sanctification and immortal blessedness depend." We listen, not "with venerating faith," but with profound aversion and distress. As I have proved in Lecture VIII. the Gospels leave no room for doubt that Jesus was condemned to be crucified only because he had made himself equal with God.

The history and records of the early Church, as given in the Acts of the Apostles, and in the Epistles of Paul, Peter, James, and Jude, all prove that the Apostles and first followers of Jesus did expect his return in the clouds to judge the world within their own generation. It is scarcely credible that such an expectation should have arisen, or been so firmly held, if Jesus himself had not given grounds for it by his own solemn declarations as recorded in the Gospels. The claim of superhuman superiority is certainly proved to have been made, and there is only one passage in the whole of the Gospels which implies any consciousness of human weakness or frailty on the part of Jesus, or any true humility. "Why callest thou me good? there is none good but one, that is God." I know that in a moment of blind infatuation Christians have quoted also the words: "I am meek and lowly of heart" as token of his humility: but this is the last thing that a really humble man could ever say of himself —"See how humble I am!" Matt. xix. 17. Matt. xi. 29.

All this self-exaltation of Christ in the Synoptics reaches a pitch of arrogance and assumption in the Fourth Gospel, which makes it so particularly offensive. My case is already really so strong that

I need not quote any more passages from the Fourth Gospel at all. The all-important question must follow: Were those claims of superiority true? Was Jesus so much more than man and so much on an equality with God as to justify him in taking the lofty tone ascribed to him by the Evangelists? If not, as the Unitarians maintain, then every effort on Christ's part to exalt himself was either a stain upon his character, or it revealed mental aberration. Both alternatives are fatal to the idea that he was a perfect or even trustworthy teacher on the sacred theme of religion.

But if, as the orthodox maintain, he was what he claimed to be, then we must make the mournful confession that as a picture of a Divine Being, he was not attractive at all, but repellent, and in a hundred ways violates our noblest conceptions of "the High and Holy One that inhabiteth eternity," the God of all love and mercy, and makes us feel how degraded and corrupt must have been the idea of Deity in the minds and hearts of those who accepted Jesus as a God. Painful to us, indeed, but not more painful than awfully untrue were those words of his, "He that hath seen me hath seen the Father."

Once more, I have proved from the Gospels that "the Deification of Jesus is the grand historical testimony to the meanness of men's thoughts about God."

Lecture XII.

We have now passed under review the salient features in the life and teachings of Jesus Christ as recorded in the Four Gospels. It was not necessary to quote every minute or isolated saying of his, but sufficient has now been quoted to give a fair representation of the picture in the Gospels. From these quotations it will be manifest that Jesus was not an infallible teacher of Divine truth, not always an immaculate example for us to follow, and therefore not entitled to hold the place of a God incarnate assigned to him by the Christians, or to deserve the extravagant eulogies poured out upon him by Dr. Martineau and by those who think and speak of Jesus in the same strain.

My work this morning will be much more pleasing than heretofore, to myself at least, if not also to my hearers. I wish to show wherein I admire both the character of Jesus and his teachings. Many persons have been so angry with me for pointing out the errors and blemishes at all (as if, indeed, I could possibly be blameworthy for calling attention to anything which the Gospels contain) that they falsely imagine I have no reverence or eulogy for that which is good. They quite forget that I admire the excellences of Jesus quite as much as they do: that, in fact, my strong admiration for what is good and lovely is at the bottom of all my criticism of the Christ of the Gospels, and renders it not only profitable but necessary. I say we cannot truly admire the beauties in the character and words of Jesus without deprecating the unlovely and misleading features. That would be only a sham homage at best, which would dishonour the object of veneration by openly refusing to look closely into the portrait given of him in the Gospels.

And what I have to say this morning, you may be sure, comes from my heart. I am not moved to speak in praise of Jesus by any of his promises, or by any of his threats. I have no purpose in the world to serve but the honest expression of my own feelings in regard to Jesus. I only express them for what they are worth. My impressions of his character may err through defect or through excess. I can only say just what I think and feel.

First, I see in Jesus, without doubt, a truly pious soul, showing a piety not touched or shaken by any errors or mistakes, piety which consisted in real consciousness of personal relations to a loving Father in heaven, whom he trusted and loved, and tried his best to obey. Search the Gospels through and not a word can you find to cast a shadow on this true piety of Jesus. It is only to be regretted that so few of his prayers are recorded, that not a single Psalm of Praise which he may have used has come down to us, and that the only two instances in which the words of his thanks to God are recorded would have been far better left out. In spite of all this, from first to last Jesus stands before me as a truly religious and pious soul.

<small>Matt. xi 25 John xi. 41, 42.</small>

Secondly: My next impression is that, in consequence of his true piety, he was unquestionably sincere—to use his own expression, he had a "single eye"—he was always straightforward, and not turned for one moment from his honest purpose by any motives of expediency or worldly prudence; but shewed—if I may use the expression without being misunderstood—a divine recklessness of consequences to himself, in the faithful discharge of what he thought to be his duty. And, my friends, we want a great deal more of this spirit of Christ in our own day. We are hampered at every turn by motives of expediency, by worldliness—worldliness in ourselves, worldliness in others. We are not sufficiently carried away by a holy zeal, but are fettered and lowered by our regard for social and other advantages, which Christ's simplicity and divine recklessness of consequences puts utterly to shame. You never see him sordid, you never see him calculating how he may win the favour of men, nor how he may shun their reproach. With all his egregious mistakes, he was a thoroughly honest man; and because he was honest, he was brave, and we should all do better if we were more like him in this respect. And here again we find the Gospels all but unanimous in their testimony to his deep sincerity and honesty and singlemindedness;

<small>Matt. vi. 22, 23.</small>

the only exceptions being where he tells his disciples that he speaks in parables only to mislead the common people: and where, at the raising of Lazarus, he openly proclaimed his own insincerity by saying that he thanked God only for the bystanders to hear him—which is too absurd to be believed. So I prefer to take the almost unexceptional testimony of the Gospels to the utter integrity and honesty of Jesus.

<small>Mark iv. 11.</small>

<small>John xi. 41, 42.</small>

Thirdly, I admire the attitude which he took in regard to the possession of this world's goods. Personally, he chose the life of a mendicant (not an example for us to follow), which certainly involved hardships; sometimes he had not where to lay his head. If he hungered, he would not ask his Father to turn stones into bread for him; he scorned the idea that men could live by bread alone; and never said anything more true than this, "A man's life consisteth not in the abundance of things which he possesseth." He advised men to seek after the riches that never fade, "where neither moth nor rust doth corrupt, and where thieves do not break through nor steal." He shewed also how grievously the love of riches and the hankering after the good things of life destroy the soul's integrity, blind the eyes to truth, and sooner or later make a dreadful gulf between the soul and God. "Take heed and beware of covetousness." "No man can serve two masters. Ye cannot serve God and Mammon." Every bit of this teaching is good and true, and needs constant

<small>Luke xii. 15.</small>

<small>Matt. vi. 20.</small>

<small>Luke xii. 15.</small>
<small>Matt. vi. 24.</small>

repetition in this and in every age. But, of course, I do not admire much of his language concerning riches and rich men. It was grounded on a profound ignorance of the true value of wealth and of the indispensable necessity of wealth being stored up and safeguarded by some men for the very sustenance of the poor. In spite of all the evils which have arisen through the wrong methods of gaining wealth and through the bad and selfish purposes to which wealth has been put, wealth has still been the very salvation of the poor. For unless some people had been rich, the poor would have been the first to suffer, and a thousand times worse off than they were. In this light riches have a moral value, and the gaining of them is a righteous pursuit, and not to be condemned wholesale in the unwise words of Christ. In many passages, and in the Parable of the Rich Man and Lazarus, he rails at the rich simply because they are rich, as if it were a crime to be rich. Nevertheless, the spirit of true brotherly service of our fellow-men by all the good gifts we enjoy is one which may be fostered by some other of Christ's words; and to live in the spirit of these words will at least keep us from becoming slaves to a lust for gold, and keep our minds and hearts from the terrible danger of covetousness. With Jesus, worldly advantage was never the thing uppermost or even present to his mind, and I respectfully commend this spirit to both the rich and the poor in this age. It is better for themselves and for each other to put Duty first

Luke vi. 24.
Mark x. 23.
Luke xvi. 19-31.

and foremost, to keep sympathy and brotherly love ever uppermost in all our thoughts and words and deeds, to "care more," as we say in our Service of Benediction, to "care more to serve well than to receive much." And I repeat that there is still plenty to learn from the personal attitude of Jesus towards worldly good.

Fourthly, I admire with unfeigned respect his attitude towards outcasts, publicans, harlots, and low people in general. There was a total absence here of self-righteousness and that feeling of moral superiority which is expressed so tersely by the words: "Stand by, for I am holier than thou." I am not saying that exact imitation of him in these days is practicable at all, or even desirable, because it might do far more harm than good. But it strikes me that the spirit at the bottom of it is very much wanted indeed in our times, I mean the spirit of feeling that we are all children of one Father God, all alike on the level of poor sinners, which makes our contact with all sorts and conditions of men one of true respect and sympathy and brotherly love, and of that pity which is akin to love and not akin to contempt. There ought to be no outcasts. To be an outcast at all is almost for a man or woman to be turned into a devil. To be an outcast, to know how one is looked down upon, shunned and loathed by the so-called good and respectable, is to kindle within a human soul the worst passions of the wild beast. We have never tried it, never known what it is to be shuddered at and shrunk from as a pestilent thing. We cannot have the faintest idea of its misery or of the depth of evil which such a feeling inspires—especially when it is felt to be partly deserved. No wonder it drives the tainted flock together in a new bond of infamy and hatred of all that is good. No wonder it leads to gross intemperance and other forms of vice, and to still grosser shamelessness and loss of every vestige of self-respect. And few there are who ever contemplate the awful danger to Society thus brought on by Society's dainty and cruel contempt. Very few are aware that the presence of such classes, bereft of all human care and sympathy, is a horrible volcano which one day will burst in fury over our boasted civilization. But unless the plague be stayed, the catastrophe will fall. Unless our wives and daughters, as well as our clergy and a few philanthropists, come to the rescue of their outcast sisters (too often brought to a life of shame by their own husbands and sons and brothers), the judgment will assuredly overtake us, and the God and Father of us all will awaken us by the solemn appeal, "Where is thy sister? Her blood crieth out unto me from the ground." In these days of hypocrisy, it is thought outrageous even to hint at such poor outcasts in the pulpit. But Jesus in his simplicity, his purity and his sympathy, not only talked about them but talked with them; nay, went among them as an equal, sat down to eat and to drink with them, not going to them with gloves on, or with patronizing airs of superior virtue, but just treating

Genesis iv. 9-18.

them as sisters and friends—with but one pure and divine hope in his breast, viz.: to lift them out of the mire and to redeem them from their shame. It will be said that all this, of course, is out of the question in our day. And if we wanted to do it, we should not know how, we should be speechlessly, helplessly, incapable of doing it. But the undying, inextinguishable spirit is there; it is enshrined in those very fallible mendacious Gospels we have been criticising; and so long as they stand, they bear witness to the spirit which is so foreign to our own, so immeasurably higher than ours. The good deeds done will never be lost: the truth once spoken cannot perish. And in just so far as those Gospels tell us, and so simply, what Jesus did and what he said to and for the poor outcasts of his day, the world at last will have to come round, whether they like it or not, to his method of dealing with them, to his notion of driving out sin by love. We only regret that he did not shew the same brotherly love to the classes above him as to the classes below him.

Fifthly, I admire Christ for what he said concerning non-resistance of evil. And here I must pay more regard to his precepts than to his example. His teaching aimed at the principle of overcoming evil with good. He would have us never feel resentment, and therefore never indulge in revenge. He began by telling us to "love" even our enemies, to bless them which curse us, and to pray for them who despitefully use and persecute

Matt. v. 44.

us. He proclaims that the spirit of resentment, the spirit of always standing on our rights, is wrong. He would have us return benefit for injury, kindness for tyranny and cruelty. In short, he goes straight against our natural and ready feelings of revenge, and tells us to root them out. Some of his language on this point, if taken literally, would do more harm than good. But the spirit of the injunction is always right, and just what we need to correct the glaring fault which is so universal and so inveterate. God knows I would not boast, but I have so admired this part of Christ's teaching as to try my best to follow it, and have often got sneered at by other people as being both weak and foolish. I find it so hard to practise, that I am convinced how far we have to travel before we reach so high a standard. But surely it is worth while trying, whenever we are injured or ill-served, to make kind excuses if we can; to look, if possible, at the good points in the character and conduct of the person who has offended us. It is surely worth while also to remember our own frailties and sins whenever we feel called upon to rebuke the shortcomings and faults of others.

Sixthly: Closely akin to this doctrine of non-resistance, is the forgiveness of those who trespass against us. It must needs be that offences come, but Jesus teaches us to forgive and be at peace with one another as soon as possible. He reminds us that a state of enmity chokes our very prayers, and we cannot hope to feel reconciled

Matt. v. 23, 24.

to God while we are not reconciled to our brother. We too often excuse ourselves by the frequency of the offence which annoys us. We say in our impatience: "There! that is what you are always saying or doing to annoy me"—as if that could justify our resentment! Peter asked Jesus, "How often shall my brother sin against me and I forgive him—till seven times? Jesus answered him, I say not unto thee till seven times, but until seventy times seven." Is not this rare and delicious? Is it not a picture of serenity, patience, forbearance, and goodwill, that any kind heart would long to resemble? It is indeed beautiful, and but for our nasty pride we should oftener try to copy it. In the narratives of the Gospels we regret to find, especially in the Fourth Gospel, threatenings of Jesus against those who offended or rejected him, out of all harmony with his own beautiful teachings; yet this blemish is greatly redeemed by his words on the cross, "Father forgive them, for they know not what they do!"

<small>Matt. xviii. 21-22.</small>

<small>Luke xxiii. 34.</small>

There are other and minor sayings of Christ which I might quote also for approval. But on these six points I utterly admire the spirit of Jesus as conveyed partly in his conduct and partly in his sayings. It remains for me only to remind you that out of the six points enumerated, five are systematically neglected by his professed disciples in general. Of course there are exceptions; but as a rule, single-mindedness, strict integrity of thought and speech, unworldliness, disregard of social position and contempt for popularity, brotherly treatment of the outcasts and depraved, non-resistance and the returning of good for evil, and finally the full and free forgiveness of aggravated offences, are virtues and nobilities of character which the Christian Church has seldom cultivated, and in which Christians generally are conspicuously deficient. So much for calling Christ "Lord, Lord," and yet making little or no effort to follow that which in his precepts, character and conduct was really good! No doubt somebody will call me uncharitable, but I reckon with certainty on the mass of thoughtful and good-hearted Christian men and women joining with me in my lament that these all-important elements in human welfare and social improvement do not receive the attention which they deserve. These excellences were, I believe, the chief cause of the spread of early Christianity among the Gentile population of the Roman Empire. When they ceased to predominate, a base and corrupt form of Christianity took its place, and went into open partnership with the idolatry and immoral principles of the pagan world. Before our own world can be purged of this idolatry and corruption, we shall have to learn the highest lessons of personal piety to the One Living and Loving God, integrity, unselfishness, and brotherly love, and, in the admirable words of Jesus, try to be perfect, "even as our Father in heaven is Matt. v. 48. perfect."

Lecture XIII.

We have now quoted sufficiently from the Four Gospels to show the conflicting and contradictory character of the teachings of Jesus Christ; how, in fact, he did teach some beautiful Theistic truths, and how also he spoiled and subverted and destroyed them by the great bulk of his subsequent teaching. In arguing with Unitarians, who still claim that Jesus was the greatest teacher of the Fatherhood of God, we must admit with them that the Gospels are not trustworthy, that we cannot rely on their absolute accuracy in any report of the sayings of Jesus; and that, in particular, the Fourth Gospel is less likely to report faithfully what Jesus said than the other three Gospels. We and our opponents also know that there is no other book to which we can refer to tell us truly what Jesus said, or to throw any light upon the darkness and confusion of the whole problem.

Still, there is one source of evidence which we have not yet consulted, and which may serve more or less to lead us to form a correct conclusion as to the main features of Christ's teaching. This source of evidence is to be found in the teaching of the Apostles and immediate followers of Jesus Christ.

We may ask, Since these men are more likely than any one else to have known what Jesus taught, and also were sure to reveal unconsciously the strongest impression made upon them by Jesus, what can we learn from their testimony? What formed the essence of their teaching and message to the world? Was it a purely Theistic teaching? Did the Apostles and first preachers of the Gospel talk wholly or even chiefly of the fatherly love of God towards all men? Did they pray after the manner in which it is asserted in the Gospels Jesus taught them to pray? Did they never mention Christ as a mediator between God and man? Did they never even faintly or remotely declare that God's forgiveness of sins depended on the death of Jesus Christ on their behalf? Did they never allude to the office of Judge, which their Saviour was to hold? Did they never repeat the threatenings which Jesus had uttered in his lifetime against those who disbelieved his claims?

But if we find, on searching over the ground of the *Acts of the Apostles* and the Epistles alleged to have been written by the intimate companions of Jesus, namely, Peter, James, John and Jude (if indeed John, the author of the Epistles, may be included among them at all)—if we find that they one and all teach scarcely any pure Theism, but a corrupt and degraded form of religious belief such as we find in the bulk of the teachings of Jesus in the Gospels, we have then the strongest proof we can get that those sayings of Jesus which Theists and Unitarians disapprove are quite as likely to be genuine and to have been uttered by him as those few of a purely Theistic character; indeed, we may go further and say that we have herein a proof of what I have been maintaining all along, viz., that whatever good might have been done by the earlier teaching of Jesus about the Fatherhood of God (and which he inherited as a Jew) was altogether undone by what he said afterwards; insomuch that the nearest of his disciples betray the injurious influence of those later teachings upon themselves. St. Paul I leave out of the category, for the simple reason that he knew nothing of Jesus personally, and that he preached and wrote under the influence and with the help only of second-hand reports of what Jesus said and did. His theology, based chiefly on the fall of man and the primæval curse, cannot find any parallel in the teaching of Jesus, while the atonement itself is only once or twice referred to in the Synoptics, and does not come into any prominence till the Fourth Gospel; so that we must not blame Jesus at all for the principal foundations of St. Paul's doctrine. With the other four Apostles whom I mentioned, the case is wholly different. If any persons in the world ought to have known what Christ wished them to preach, it would be they to whom Jesus solemnly said, "Unto you it is given to know the mysteries of the kingdom of heaven, but to them it is not given." If I refer to the *Acts of the Apostles*, it is because it is the stronghold of the traditional party and the foundation of the impious claims

<small>Matt. xiii. 11.</small>

of sacerdotalism. The Apostles are represented as equal, or nearly equal, to Jesus Christ himself, in holding a Divine authority and being infallible teachers of men. For my part, I regard the book as very untruthful and misleading, and, while professing to be historical, it gives in many parts a flat contradiction to the best authenticated Epistle of Paul—viz., to the Galatians. It begins with a brazen repetition of what we find in the Fourth Gospel about the sending of the Holy Ghost, and that this third God would give the Apostles power to be witnesses, not for God, but for Christ. On the day of Pentecost, after Peter had been proclaiming the exaltation of Christ to the right hand of God, the people cried out, "Men and brethren, what shall we do? Then Peter said unto them, Repent and be baptised every one of you in the name of Jesus Christ for the remission of sins." Peter heals a lame man at the temple gate, using these words, "Silver and gold have I none; but such as I have, I give thee: in the name of Jesus Christ of Nazareth, rise up and walk." This was followed by a short sermon all about Jesus Christ, misquoting the Old Testament prophecies as referring to him, whereas they never refer to him at all. Go on to the next chapter, and the next, and all through, and you will find no Theistic utterances by Peter save one, "Of a truth I perceive that God is no respecter of persons, but in every nation he that feareth God and worketh righteousness is accepted with Him." In chapter v. there is the

_{Acts ii. 37, 38.}

_{Acts iii. 6.}

_{Acts x. 34, 35.}

horrible story of Ananias and Sapphira, written in honour of the Apostles *and* the Holy Ghost, who is made to share the discredit of it with them. Stephen, before his death, said: "Behold, I see the heavens opened, and the Son of Man standing on the right hand of God," and he died praying: "Lord Jesus, receive my spirit." Jesus Christ and the Holy Ghost are the two objects perpetually before the minds and upon the lips of these Apostles. And when Paul comes upon the scene he too takes up the same theme, and in answer to the cry of the gaoler at Philippi, "What must I do to be saved?" says, "Believe on the Lord Jesus Christ and thou shalt be saved." I only introduce Paul's teaching here because it is reported in the *Acts of the Apostles*. I do not quote from his own Epistles. In his celebrated sermon on Mar's Hill he preached some eight verses of pure Theism, quoting from the Greek poet Cleanthes, "We are the offspring of God." But even this sermon he spoilt by talking about "that man" whom God had ordained to judge the world. At Lystra, when the people wanted to offer the sacrifices to them, Paul also taught a few words of pure Theism. With these rare exceptions the Apostles are reported as teaching what I have called the corruption of Theism which Jesus himself is reported as teaching in the Gospels. If Jesus was not to blame for the Apostolic error, I do not know who was, for they were all born Jews. But I reserve for the last this passage. "And when they agreed not among themselves they departed, after that Paul had spoken one word, Well spake the Holy Ghost by Esaias the Prophet unto our fathers, saying, Go unto this people and say, Hearing, ye shall hear and shall not understand; and seeing, ye shall see and not perceive; for the heart of this people is waxed gross, and their ears are dull of hearing, and their eyes have they closed; lest they should see with their eyes and hear with their ears and understand with their heart, and should be converted and I should heal them." These words, or words like them, are imputed to Jesus himself in all the Four Gospels, and in Mark with especial obnoxiousness, where Jesus is made to say that *he* is the wanton cause of the blindness Mark iv. 12. and dulness of heart, and that he speaks in parables only to mislead.

We must now turn to the Epistles of Peter, James, John and Jude. There is great beauty in the First Epistle of Peter, manifest in the spirit of holiness and love and steadfastness which he inculcates. He also recognises God the Father, and gives thanks to Him for the redemption through Christ. But when this has been admitted, we are forced to say that the rest of the Epistle is not Theistic at all, but teems throughout with the eulogies of the precious blood of Christ as a ransom or price paid for the redemption of the elect. He exalts Christ into the position of a mediator and intercessor, and makes him, if not equal with God, at least " on the right hand of God, angels and authorities and powers 1 Peter iii. 22. being made subject unto him." He repeats the

1 Peter iii. 21. false teaching of Christ about the saving power of baptism. He also emphatically expresses his belief
1 Peter iv. 5. that Jesus is coming speedily to judge the quick and the dead.

The Epistle of James is also full of moral excellence and beauty, but he, too, exalts Christ to the
James ii. 1. position of "the Lord of Glory," and adopts the Apostolic notion of the miraculous efficacy of the
James v. 14, 15. Name of the Lord. "Is any sick among you, let him call for the elders of the Church, and let them pray over him, anointing him with oil in the name of the Lord; and the prayer of faith shall save the sick, and the Lord shall raise him up; and if he have committed sins, they shall be forgiven him." The orthodox Christians deem it an eccentric folly to obey this Apostolic injunction, and call the people who obey it by the name they adopted, viz., "The Peculiar People." St. James also believes in the near approach of the second coming of Christ
James v. 8, 9. to judge the world. "The coming of the Lord draweth nigh." "Behold, the judge standeth before the door." In all other respects his Epistle is mainly Theistic.

If we turn now to the Epistles of John, we find them written in the style of the Fourth Gospel. It is, indeed, almost impossible to doubt that the author of the Gospel is the author of the Epistles also. Hence we find Jesus put on a level with God the Father. We find also the atonement by blood
John i. 7. continually repeated. "The blood of Jesus Christ his Son cleanseth us from all sin." Those beautiful

Theistic words. "If we confess our sins, he is faithful and just to forgive us our sins," are spoilt almost immediately by his saying, "If any man sin, we have an advocate with the Father, Jesus Christ the righteous: and he is the propitiation for our sins, and not for ours only, but also for the sins of the whole world." "God sent His only-begotten Son into the world, that we might live through him. Herein is love, not that we loved God, but that He loved us, and sent His Son to be the propitiation for our sins." John dwells on the necessity for believing and confessing that Jesus is the Son of God, and makes much of the sacramental mystery of the water and the blood. "He that hath the Son hath life, and he that hath not the Son of God hath not life." He alludes to the unpardonable sin spoken of by Jesus, "There is a sin unto death. I do not say that he shall pray for it." "He that abideth in the doctrine of Christ, he hath both the Father and the Son. If there come any unto you and bring not this doctrine, receive him not into your house, neither bid him God-speed: for he that biddeth him God-speed is partaker of his evil deeds."

1 John i. 9.
1 John ii. 1, 2.
1 John iv. 9, 10.
1 John v. 12
1 John v. 16.
2 John 9-11.

Jude's Epistle is characterised by a recognition of Jesus as the Lord and Judge: he quotes from the book of Enoch, which appeared shortly before the time of Christ, "Behold the Lord cometh with ten thousand of his saints, to execute judgment, etc." He believes in the mediation of Christ, "Keep yourselves in the love of God, looking for the mercy of our Lord Jesus Christ unto eternal life." The

Jude 14.
Jude 21.

Jude 24, 25. ascription of praise in the last verses used to be regarded as given to Jesus, and not to God the Father: "Now unto Him who is able to keep you from falling, and to present you faultless before the presence of His glory with exceeding joy; to the only wise God our Saviour be glory and majesty, dominion and power, both now and ever. Amen." In the Revised Version, however, the words "through Jesus Christ our Lord" have now been interpolated, on the authority of the Sinaitic, Vatican, and Alexandrian MSS.

I might quote also the Book of Revelation as the work of the beloved disciple, the Apostle John, *Mark iii. 17.* whom Jesus called a Son of Thunder. But the identification of him with the author of this book is not complete, and therefore its contents would not be evidence of the personal influence of the teaching of Jesus.

On the whole, then, we may be quite sure that the non-Theistic teachings of Christ had the strongest influence on the minds of his immediate followers; and that they were deeply impregnated with a belief in his claims to be equal with God, and the appointed judge of all men at the last day. They all agree in believing in the Devil, all agree in believing in the mediatorial work of Christ, and, with the exception of James, all agree in believing that the blood of Jesus Christ was a ransom paid for the redemption of the elect, and as a propitiation for the sins of men. All except St. James make the condition of salvation depend on believing in

Jesus Christ as a Saviour. All except John expect the speedy return of Christ to earth to judge the world. And although all the three, Peter, James and John, occasionally say things which are agreeable to the Theistic faith, yet none teach the true Fatherhood of God over all men without alloy, except in one fine passage: "Wherefore let them that suffer according to the will of God, commit the keeping of their souls to Him in well-doing, as unto a faithful Creator." If St. Paul's writings were to be included among this evidence — which they ought not to be, considering he never knew Jesus at all during his lifetime — the departure from the Theistic sayings of Jesus would appear just as great, if not greater, on all essential points.

Hence it is not to be wondered at that the Early Church as it grew should recede further and further from the simplicity of *e.g.* the Lord's Prayer, and the other few cognate sentences uttered by Jesus in the Sermon on the Mount and in the parable of the Prodigal Son. The Church dogmas are for the most part fairly drawn from the Gospels, representing in about the same proportion the Theistic and the non-Theistic elements. But in practice the dogmas are not consistently adhered to, some receiving more attention and regard in one age and less in another, so that when they contradict one another, one set of beliefs must necessarily be upheld at the expense of another set. Let me illustrate this. The Nicene Creed begins: — "I believe in one God the Father, Almighty, Maker of heaven and earth, and of all things visible and invisible." But immediately goes on to say:— "And in one Lord Jesus Christ, the only-begotten Son of God; begotten of his Father before all worlds; God of God, Light of Light, Very God of Very God, begotten not made, being of one substance with the Father: By whom (*i.e.*, Jesus) all things were made." Here you have a distinct assertion of only one God, one Maker of all things immediately followed by a distinct assertion of another God, another Maker, besides the first-named. So in one age the first God might be worshipped and glorified more than the second. In another age, as now, the second God will be worshipped and glorified more than the first. For this creed makes no pretence of a doctrine of a Trinity. It is a bold and bare assertion of three Gods, or at least of two. The Unitarian cannot throw stones at the orthodox Christians for repeating what Jesus Christ himself taught them to believe, unless he lays aside the empty boast that Jesus was pre-eminently the teacher of the true and universal Fatherhood of God. Jesus only taught it as the Nicene Creed teaches it, merely in words, to knock it down in the next breath. As an advocate for Jesus, I am speechless before those Four Gospels. I dare not claim him as a Theist, because I see what a far greater mass of evidence the Gospels contain to shew that he was *not*.

I think it only right to remind you that in these Lectures on the teachings of Jesus Christ I have not made any accusations which I have not proved by quotations from his own words. When I am reproached for attacking Christ, it is almost ludicrous to see what the reproach amounts to. It means to imply that I cannot do Jesus Christ a greater wrong than to repeat and to call attention to what he himself said or to what his nearest and dearest friends have reported as his own words. If that be any injury or dishonour to him, it is not my fault, surely, but that of himself or of his nearest friends.

But I hope, as I have done this work out of a sense of duty, and with an honest desire to get at the facts, my labour will not be wholly lost, but may possibly awaken earnest thought in the minds of those who have hitherto been honest and true-hearted believers in Christ because, and only because, they thought that God their Maker wished them to be so. No fidelity to Him can ever finally lose its reward.

Lecture XIV.

I AM compelled to supplement my thirteen Lectures on Jesus Christ by another, in order to meet some objections which have been made to them. In doing this I am not at all, or even chiefly, concerned to vindicate myself. In this matter I do not consider myself able to judge of the wisdom or the folly of my action as it appears and can only appear in the sight of God. "I judge not mine own self," as St. Paul said, "but He that judgeth me is the Lord." In doing as I have done, I sought neither for human praise nor blame, though expecting blame as a matter of course. The sole object I have in answering objections at all is to give to the hearers and readers of these Lectures fresh ground, if needful, for seeing the necessity of such work being done.

<small>1 Cor. iv. 3-4.</small>

The list of objections opens as usual with a general condemnation of all controversy, and especially of controversy carried on in a church. To this objection there is a very simple answer, and I think it ought to suffice. The Theistic Church was set on foot, and has been marvellously supported for nearly a quarter of a century, to teach and to proclaim certain higher and truer thoughts concerning God and His dealings, and His relations to mankind; these higher thoughts being in open opposition to the creeds of Christendom, and to what is still widely believed and taught in orthodox churches and chapels. If our hearts are deeply stirred with the love of God, and desire to make it felt also in the world at large; if we deem it a solemn duty, a sacred privilege, to make these Theistic teachings known among men, we must do as all teachers are compelled to do if they desire to teach anything at all. To the purely unsophisticated, to the minds which are a perfect blank, to those who have never had any teaching about God, true or false, there is obviously only one duty, viz.: to teach them the simple truth so far as we know it, and to keep off the very breath of controversy. For little children, and for men and women who may be in exactly their state of unbiassed or unprejudiced mind, controversy would be entirely superfluous and misplaced. But these conditions do not prevail, the contrary conditions prevail. Even our little children are liable to be contaminated, and in fact are contaminated, with the errors which fill the air, which are heard in every school they may attend, and are repeated and babbled by their schoolmates and playmates. And if this be so with our children, we need not lay any more emphasis on the fact that men and women are in the same condition—exposed to, if not already steeped in, Christian creeds and traditions which are deeply hostile to Theism, and must be removed if Theism is ever to prevail and to supersede them.

This fact makes controversy a religious duty in no wise to be evaded, but to be manfully carried on at the cost of any amount of personal annoyance and self-sacrifice. To take an old and familiar illustration of the need for controversy; if any one has been taught that $2 \times 2 = 5$ you must not only tell him and show him that $2 \times 2 = 4$, but controversially point out that if the latter be true, the former is false. If you do not do that, he will not learn the truth, he will remain under the impression that both results are equally true, or that it does not matter what the product of 2×2 may be.

As to the propriety or impropriety of carrying on controversy in a church, much depends on the quantity and the quality of it, and also on the spirit in which it is conducted. If it be aimed spitefully against persons, it is outrageously wrong, and would be wrong anywhere; but if aimed only at errors of opinion and belief, errors which mislead the mind and corrupt the heart, it is both edifying and helpful; for that which helps the mind to discern intellectual truth more clearly, helps, at the same time, to win the heart and to enlist its energies in the cause of righteousness. If any of you, my friends, can get no good out of such controversy as is carried on here, I venture to suggest that it may be your own fault, possibly due to your own lack of discernment that controversy is part of the work to be done for God and His truth, possibly due to your own lack of hatred of falsehood, your own lack of indignation against those errors and superstitions which are hiding the face of God from the Christian world. If you did but feel the danger and the pernicious influences of ancient error upon the minds and hearts of the present generation, you would be thankful to hear the word of warning uttered and the extreme peril pointed out. No doubt, in your heart you abhor priestcraft, or at all events you abhor the vile abuses to which it gives rise. I ask, Have you ever steadfastly looked at the only belief which makes priestcraft possible, and covers its abominations with a veil of sanctity? The belief in the Godhead of Christ is the sole foundation of all that gigantic evil. The priest claims to stand in the place of Christ; and Christ, he asserts, was a God, and gave his authority to the priests to claim and to exercise complete control over men and women. Nothing will destroy this arrogance and prevent its further mischief but the uprooting of the belief in the Godhead of Christ. If there were no other reason, this of itself would necessitate the controversy to which you object. It is worth remembering too that, while controversy which is aimed at Christian error and superstition is deprecated and denounced, the same objectors have no word of complaint to make when the controversy is aimed against Atheism and Agnosticism. It is only when the fictitious Christ of the Gospels is held up for criticism that any objection to controversy is raised. As to the effect of controversy being bad on some minds, I can only observe that, like all we do and say, this also will help some and hinder others. We cannot avoid this. It is a consequence of the diversity of men's minds and moods—not only one mind differing from another, but the same mind having diverse moods and deriving benefit at one time from that which is, or seems to be, harmful at another. The objection to these lectures being delivered in a church is further disposed of by recollecting the purpose of them. They were not designed nor composed as a mere string of intellectual propositions, but as a necessary and indispensable part of the training of our consciences and hearts. The conscience of Christendom has been deeply blurred through its blindness to the moral blemishes of the Christ of the Gospels. The heart of Christendom has been deeply injured by taking for a God a very imperfect and mistaken man. The object of these Lectures was intensely religious, and therefore most appropriate to the hour of worship. If a single soul, formerly enslaved by the Christian idolatry, left this church, after one of these Lectures on Jesus Christ, distinctly shaken in his belief in Christ's infallibility as a man and as a teacher of religious truth; if a single soul was moved by the exposure of the contents of the Gospels to go up higher and cling in faith and love to the Living God, the everlasting righteous Father; then I know that my course was right, then I have the proof of fact that the controversy has been been approved and blessed by God who has made it an instrument of opening blind eyes and of drawing the heart of at least one of His children to Himself. And testimony to this good effect has, to my glad surprise, been plentiful enough. If The Theistic Church is to be of any use, it must be a Church militant here on earth; fighting not against poor fallible men like ourselves, but against the vanities and lies which still prevail and exercise so fatal a tyranny over the unthinking, the young, and the cowardly. We must as a Church give bread to hungry souls, and not stones; water to the thirsty, and not poison. But we need first to strike off their fetters and open their prison doors, and give them the freedom by which alone they can eat and drink and live. For my part I do not think this Church would be doing its plain duty if it were for one moment to relax its hostility towards the rampant and tyrannous errors which the Christian Church has made alliance with the world of fashion in order to uphold. A creed that is not worth fighting for is not worth having. Conviction so weak that it would never contend or dispute for its supremacy, is no conviction at all, and in such a case it would really not matter a straw what one believed or disbelieved.

Objection has also been expressed to the line which I took, that I made little or no reference to the new historical criticism or to the influence which that and the spread of science are having upon the old dogmas. But all this would have been quite outside the scope of what I had set myself to do. The historical criticism is of the highest value in certain limited circles of scholars and thinkers; but it does not touch the real question which I sought to answer. Historical criticism does not concern itself with moral questions, or with the deepest of all—our conceptions of God and His dealings with us. My task was to show that upon the popular belief that the New Testament is absolutely trustworthy as history, the pictures of Christ in it are not at all perfect, and that some of his teachings were not right nor true. Therefore this fact would lead inevitably to the conclusion that the idea of Christ's human perfection, and the more preposterous idea of Christ's Godhead, could not be sustained so long as the Christ so imagined was identified with the Christ of the Gospels. And all this was necessarily argued on the popular belief that the Gospels are trustworthy records of what the real Jesus said and did. But my objector goes on to say that even on that ground I was wrong in arguing on the assumption that Christ was only a man, when the Christians justify to themselves all that he said and did on the assumption that he was a God. Now here it ought to be plain and intelligible that if the Gospels represent Christ as an imperfect man, *à fortiori*, he could not have been a God; for no assumption can make that to be right which is intrinsically wrong. If the record had depicted a perfect man, it would still have left an enormous gulf between that and the assumption of his Godhead. How much wider and deeper is that gulf when the human imperfections are frankly described! Instead of giving a mere opinion of my own about the Christ of the Gospels, I simply let the Gospels speak for themselves, and only pointed out the blemishes which they record. I did not invent any of them. And every one of the Christian advocates, critics and all, even Dr. Martineau and Unitarians, need to be re-reminded of and forced to look at those blemishes, in order to clear their minds and hearts from a false sentiment about Christ which has done, and is still doing, a world of mischief. And even were there no blemishes in the Christ at all, the supposition that he was a manifestation or revelation of God to man is in itself deeply harmful, is to erect a barrier or veil between our souls and God, takes its rise out of the idea of an absent or distant or alienated God, who has to send some one here to represent Him, and thus hides the truth that God is ever nigh to every uplifted soul, hides the truth that God, as pure spirit, is the only Being in the universe with whom the soul of man can come into immediate contact and communion; and by thus hiding the truth, the idea of incarnation puts God far away and shuts out the light of His countenance from us. It is fortunate, most fortunate, that we have in the Christ of the Gospels such an imperfect and misled human being, because it makes it all the easier to displace him from the obstructive position in which the idolatry of Christendom has placed him.

I am reproached also for not paying due heed to the Eastern hyperbole of many of the sayings on the lips of the Christ of the Gospels. Now and again I have mentioned this in defence of some of his beautiful precepts and counsels, *e.g.*, "Resist not evil," "Take no thought for the morrow." But on the whole the Gospels are very prosaic indeed. There is comparatively little resort to metaphor, and none to hyperbole, in such matters as the division of mankind into the saved and lost, the belief in devils and the endless duration of the wrath of God. On all such matters no deductions can be fairly demanded for Eastern modes of speech. No doubt, when the Gospels were written the Evangelists had no idea that they were ascribing to their master deeds and words which subsequent ages would condemn. The author of the Fourth Gospel certainly thought he was describing how the real God would speak and act if he were incarnate in a man. We are grateful indeed for the blunders into which he fell, and which make us reject his portrait of the Divine-man as nothing better than a caricature. It was time that somebody, in a religious frame of mind and with a pure regard for the interests of true religion, should demand the attention of the Christian world to what the writers of the Gospels themselves say of their own Christ. I have tried to do this to the best of my ability, in spite of the extreme unpleasantness of the task.

There remains but one more objection which I feel bound to meet. It is written in these words:—

"In accusing Christians of idolatry you misrepresent them, because it is not a man whom they worship, but God manifested as a man,"

For the present let me be supposed to withdraw the term "idolatry." I will assume that it is the wrong term to apply to the condition of heart and mind in which I see the Christians generally to be.

That condition is two-fold, negative and positive. *Negatively*, it is a practical ignoring of Him whom they call in their creeds "One God, the Father Almighty, Maker of heaven and earth." It is the absence of all confidence and trust in that God, unless they are shielded from Him by a mediator whose blood has rescued them from God's wrath. It is the refusal or the inability to pray to that God, that Father in Heaven, in the manner and in the spirit in which Jesus taught the multitudes to pray in the Sermon on the Mount. It is the absence of a total surrender of the heart's love to that God and Father, who is either not loved at all, or has only a little share of love divided between Him and the rival Christ, who, according to the Christian creeds, has done so much more than God the Father to deserve the love of men.

Positively, the condition is one of absolute worship and homage of an historical person believed to have been a God on earth. A perfect trust in Christ because God the Father is not trustworthy. A perfect love for Christ because he is far more worthy of love than "God out of Christ." It involves also a conviction that as Christ is the sole author of salvation, unless he is believed in and worshipped as a God, men cannot be saved. And inasmuch as the only historical records of Christ contain blemishes, errors in theology and errors in ethics, the Christians are really taking an imperfect man for their God, a man whose faults and errors they can see, if they choose, as well as I can; and so, without due reflection, they are accepting as their ideal of God, one who is below the highest ideal of a perfect man. You may not choose to call this idolatry. Call it then what you will. It is at least to be regarded as both wrong and dangerous, and depraving to its votaries in many ways, which the history of Christendom shows down to this hour. I have called it idolatry, and I do so again now, but I will not dispute about words and names. It is *the thing* which I hate, and in which lies man's greatest enemy and peril.

My idea of idolatry is this, but I do not consider it an exact definition, only a rough sketch. Idolatry seems to me to consist in clinging to a lower conception of God, after a higher one has been distinctly seen. It is choosing the lower and rejecting the higher. Now this is just what the Christian Churches have done. In the Gospels (not to speak of the Old Testament at all), Christ sets before us two contradictory conceptions of God, one truer and higher, and the other false and low. One, that of a loving and righteous Father of all men; the other, that of an inexorable and capricious God of endless wrath, whose wrath can only be quenched by the blood of His Son. If the second of these two contradictory conceptions of God had been the only one ever presented to the Christian mind by Jesus or by anyone else, no blame of idolatry could have been laid at their door. They knew no better and they had no choice. But the former picture was there likewise from the beginning. It was Jesus Christ's own simple Jewish religion, which he learnt at his mother's knee, and which he sometimes taught. But the Christian Church would not look at it, scorned it, and in its place either adopted Christ's lower conception of God, or created it for themselves and then ascribed it to him and put it on his lips. Every time the "Lord's Prayer" is repeated, there is a chance for Christians to repent of their idolatry, and to turn to the Living Loving God. But even the authority of Christ is not enough to wean them from it, because, you see, they have his authority for the idolatry too. There are the texts, quite as plain and much more frequent than the texts about the One God and Father of all.

If idolatry were to be defined as worshipping a conception of God lower than the true conception, all men would be idolaters, every one of us, every Jew, every Theist, as well as every Christian; because none of our highest human conceptions of God are true enough or good enough to represent the reality of what God is. We are only free from idolatry so long as we remember this and in our deepest hearts are convinced that we do not and cannot know God as He really is, on earth below. The sublimest thought about God ever put into words is that grand impersonation we find in Isaiah.

^{Isaiah lv. 8, 9.} "My thoughts are not your thoughts, neither are your ways my ways, saith the Lord. But as the heavens are higher than the earth, so are my ways higher than your ways, and my thoughts than your thoughts." How, then, is it possible for even the most perfect of men to be a true and full representation of God? If not, *à fortiori* the Christ of the Gospels must be unworthy of such a place as that hitherto assigned to him in Christendom.

"THE DEIFICATION OF JESUS IS THE GRAND HISTORICAL TESTIMONY TO THE MEANNESS OF MAN'S THOUGHTS ABOUT GOD."

WORKS by Rev. C. VOYSEY.

		s.	d.
The Sling and the Stone—			
Vols. I., II., III., IV.	Out of Print		
Vol. V.	ditto		
Vol. VI.	ditto		
Vol. VII., On Prophecy		5	0
Vol. VIII., On the Paternoster		4	0
Vol. IX.	Out of Print		
Vol. X., Revelation Tested on Moral Grounds		10	6
Mystery of Pain, Death and Sin. New Edition, Enlarged	Out of Print		
Defence at York, 1869		1	0
Appeal to Privy Council, 1870		1	0
Lectures on The Theistic Faith and on the Bible		1	0
Lecture on the Church of England		1	0
Lecture on Evolution		0	6
Revised Prayer Book and Hymns. Third Edition		3	6
Private and Family Prayers and Meditations		0	6
Bound Vols. of Sermons . . (Each)		7	6
Single Sermons		0	1
Dulwich Tracts		0	6
Theism: or The Religion of Common Sense		2	6
Theism as a Science		2	6
The Testimony of the Four Gospels concerning Jesus Christ		3	6

To be had of *WILLIAMS & NORGATE*, 14, *Henrietta Street, Covent Garden, W.C.;* or of the *AUTHOR,* St. *Valery, Hampstead, N.W.*

www.ingramcontent.com/pod-product-compliance
Lightning Source LLC
Chambersburg PA
CBHW032229230426
43666CB00033B/1654